Teach & Test
Reading Grade 2
Table of Contents

How to Use This Book

1. This book can be used in a home or classroom setting. Read through each unit before working with the student(s). Familiarize yourself with the vocabulary and the skills that are introduced at the top of each unit activity page. Use this information as a guide to help instruct the student(s).

2. Choose a quiet place with little or no interruptions (including the telephone). Talk with the student(s) about the purpose of this book and how you will be working as a team to prepare for standardized tests.

3. As an option, copy the unit test and give it as a pretest to identify weak areas.

4. Upon the completion of each unit, you will find a unit test. Discuss the Helping Hand strategy for test taking featured on the test. Use the example on each test as a chance to show the student(s) how to work through a problem and completely fill in the answer circle. Encourage the student(s) to work independently when possible, but this is a learning time, and questions should be welcomed. A time limit is given for each test. Instruct the student(s) to use the time allowed efficiently, looking back over the answers if possible. Tell him to continue until he sees the stop sign.

5. Record the score on the record sheet on page 4. If a student has difficulty with any questions, use the cross-reference guide on the inside back cover to identify the skills that need to be reviewed.

Teach & Test

Introduction

Now this makes sense—teaching students the skills and strategies that are expected of them before they are tested!

Many students, parents, and teachers are concerned that standardized test scores do not adequately reflect a child's capabilities. This may be due to one or more of the factors italicized below. The purpose of this book is to reduce the negative impact of these, or similar factors, on a student's standardized test scores. The goal is to target those factors and alter their effects as described.

1. *The student has been taught the tested skills but has forgotten them.* This book is divided into units that are organized similarly to second grade textbooks. Instructions for the skill itself are found at the top of each unit activity page, ensuring that the student has been exposed to each key component. The exercises include drill/practice and creative learning activities. Additional activity suggestions can be found in a star burst within the units. These activities require the student to apply the skills that they are practicing.

2. *The student has mastered the skills but has never seen them presented in a test-type format.* Ideally, the skills a student learns at school will be used as part of problem solving in the outside world. For this reason, the skills in this book, and in most classrooms, are not practiced in a test-type format. At the end of each unit in this book, the skills are specifically matched with test questions. In this way, the book serves as a type of "bridge" between the skills that the student(s) has mastered and the standardized test format.

3. *The student is inexperienced with the answer sheet format.* Depending on the standardized test that your school district uses, students are expected to fill in the answer circles completely and neatly. The unit, midway review, and final review tests will help prepare the student(s) for this process.

4. *The student may feel the anxiety of a new and unfamiliar situation.* While testing, students will notice changes in their daily routine: their classroom door will be closed with a "Testing" sign on it, they will be asked not to use the restroom, their desks may be separated, their teacher may read from a script and refuse to repeat herself, etc. To help relieve the stress caused by these changes, treat each unit test in this book as it would be treated at school by following the procedures listed below.

Stage a Test

You will find review tests midway through the book and again at the end of the book. When you reach these points, "stage a test" by creating a real test-taking environment. The procedures listed below coincide with many standardized test directions. The purpose is to alleviate stress, rather than contribute to it, so make this a serious, but calm event and the student(s) will benefit.

1. Prepare! Have the student(s) sharpen two pencils, lay out scratch paper, and use the restroom.

2. Choose a room with a door that can be closed. Ask a student to put a sign on the door that reads "Testing" and explain that no talking will be permitted after the sign is hung.

3. Direct the student(s) to turn to a specific page but not to begin until the instructions are completely given.

4. Read the instructions at the top of the page and work through the example together. Discuss the Helping Hand strategy that is featured at the top of the page. Have the student(s) neatly and completely fill in the bubble for the example. This is the child's last chance to ask for help!

5. Instruct the student(s) to continue working until the stop sign is reached. If a student needs help reading, you may read each question only once.

Helping Hand Test Strategies

The first page of each test features a specific test-taking strategy that will be helpful in working through most standardized tests. These strategies are introduced and spotlighted one at a time so that they will be learned and remembered internally. Each will serve as a valuable test-taking tool, so discuss them thoroughly.

The strategies include:

- Whisper the sounds you are making to yourself.
- If you are unsure, try each answer in the blank.
- Read all the choices before you answer.
- When you are unsure, go back and read the story again.
- More than one answer may seem correct! Be sure to compare the choices.
- Read carefully and go back to the story if you are unsure.
- Watch for key words in the story that give you clues.
- Use your time wisely. If a question seems too tough, skip it and come back to it later.

Constructed-Response Questions

You will find the final question(s) of the tests are written in a different format called constructed response. This means that students are not provided with answer choices, but are instead asked to construct their own answers. The objective of such an "open-ended" type of question is to provide students with a chance to creatively develop reasonable answers. It also provides an insight to a student's reasoning and thinking skills. As this format is becoming more accepted and encouraged by standardized test developers, students will be "ahead of the game" by practicing such responses now.

Evaluating the Tests

Two types of questions are included in each test. The unit tests and the midway review test each consist of 20 multiple-choice questions, and the final review test consists of 25 multiple-choice questions. All tests include a constructed-response question which requires the student(s) to construct and sometimes support an answer. Use the following procedures to evaluate a student's performance on each test.

1. Use the answer key found on pages 126–128 to correct the tests. Be sure the student(s) neatly and completely filled in the answer circles.

2. Record the scores on the record sheet found on page 4. If the student(s) incorrectly answered any questions, use the cross-reference guide found on the inside back cover to help identify the skills the student(s) needs to review. Each test question references the corresponding activity page.

3. Scoring the constructed-response questions is somewhat subjective. Discuss these questions with the student(s). Sometimes it is easier for the student(s) to explain the answer verbally. Help the student to record her thoughts as a written answer. If the student(s) has difficulty formulating a response, refer back to the activity pages using the cross-reference guide. Also review the star burst activity found in the unit which also requires the student(s) to formulate an answer.

4. Discuss the test with the student(s). What strategies were used to answer the questions? Were some questions more difficult than others? Was there enough time? What strategies did the student(s) use while taking the test?

Record Sheet

Record a student's score for each test by drawing a star or placing a sticker below each item number that was correct. Leave the incorrect boxes empty as this will allow you to visually see any weak spots. Review and practice those missed skills, then retest only the necessary items.

Unit 1

1	2	3	4	5	6	7	8	9	10	11	12	13	14	15	16	17	18	19	20

Unit 2

1	2	3	4	5	6	7	8	9	10	11	12	13	14	15	16	17	18	19	20

Unit 3

1	2	3	4	5	6	7	8	9	10	11	12	13	14	15	16	17	18	19	20

Unit 4

1	2	3	4	5	6	7	8	9	10	11	12	13	14	15	16	17	18	19	20

Midway Review Test

1	2	3	4	5	6	7	8	9	10	11	12	13	14	15	16	17	18	19	20

Unit 5

1	2	3	4	5	6	7	8	9	10	11	12	13	14	15	16	17	18	19	20

Unit 6

1	2	3	4	5	6	7	8	9	10	11	12	13	14	15	16	17	18	19	20

Unit 7

1	2	3	4	5	6	7	8	9	10	11	12	13	14	15	16	17	18	19	20

Unit 8

1	2	3	4	5	6	7	8	9	10	11	12	13	14	15	16	17	18	19	20

Final Review Test

1	2	3	4	5	6	7	8	9	10	11	12	13	14	15	16	17	18	19	20

21	22	23	24	25

Name

Vowels with silent partners

When two vowels are together, the first one usually makes the long sound, and the
second one is usually silent.

Look at these double vowel words: Watch for the vowel i to be followed by the silent gh:

   road   faint   night

   rōad   fāint   nīght

Circle the word that describes each picture.

1. hear / hay	2. paint / pant	3. weed / wed
4. bet / beet	5. light / lit	6. fit / fight
7. paid / pad	8. rough / right	9. cot / coat
10. coast / cost	11. beads / beds	12. met / meat
13. goat / got	14. red / read	15. tray / train

Name _____

Double vowel words   Unit 1

Remember the rule that usually works for double vowels:
The first vowel is long. The second vowel is silent.

Complete each sentence using words from the Word Bank. Read the letters in the boxes going down to find the answer to the riddle.

What goes through water but doesn't get wet? _____

mermaid	ray	reading	float	reef	manatee
creatures	eel	seaweed	beach	coast	

1. The ocean is full of beautiful ___ ___ ___ ☐ ___ ___ ___ ___ ___ .

2. Many fish and other animals hide in the ☐ ___ ___ ___ .

3. Some ocean animals feed on ___ ___ ☐ ___ ___ ___ ___ ___ .

4. Never swim near a sting___ ___ ☐ .

5. The edge of land is called the ___ ☐ ___ ___ ___ .

6. To keep your body on top of water means to ☐ ___ ___ ___ ___ .

7. A snakelike ocean animal is the ___ ___ ☐ .

8. A ___ ___ ___ ___ ___ ☐ ___ is half woman and half fish.

9. Mom and I sat in the sun ___ ___ ___ ___ ___ ___ ___ ☐ .

10. We built sandcastles on the ___ ___ ___ ___ ☐ .

11. "That's not a sea lion. It's a ___ ___ ___ ___ ☐ ___ ___ ."

Name

R-controlled vowels

When a vowel is followed by the letter r, it makes a new sound.
Try these words to hear the r-controlled vowel sounds:

car   bird   fern   church   corn

Circle the word that describes each picture.

1. park / pork	2. bride / bird	3. born / barn	4. dirt / dart
5. farm / firm	6. porch / perch	7. starve / serve	8. cord / card
9. warm / worm	10. stark / stork	11. fern / firm	12. third / tired **3rd**
13. girl / grill	14. short / shirt	15. three / thirty **30**	16. burn / born
17. press / purse	18. turn / torn	19. fur / for	20. heart / hurt

Name

Use the words in the Word Bank to complete the puzzle. The letters in the dark boxes going down will answer the riddle.

What does a rabbit use to fix his hair? _____

| curve | burn | birthday | fern | chirp |
| nurse | thirsty | church | squirt | |

Name

Vowel digraphs

Unit 1

Each of these letter combinations makes a different sound.

o͝o broom	o͞o hook	au auto	aw claw	ĕa bread

Use one of the letter combinations to complete each word.

r_____dy	sp_____l	s_____cer
y_____n	sw_____ter	sh_____k
br_____m	l_____ndry	str_____
br_____kfast	r_____f	g_____se
f_____cet	c_____l	m_____dow
p_____l	r_____d	f_____tball
f_____n	bec_____se	w_____ther
m_____se	sh_____l	f_____t

Name

Vowel diphthongs

Unit 1

Each of these letter combinations also makes a special sound.

| ou mouse | ow flower | oi coin | oy boy | ew news |

Use the words from the Word Bank to label each picture.

1.  _____	2.  _____	3.  _____	4. _____
5.  _____	6.  _____	7.  _____	8.  _____
9.  _____	10.  _____	11.  _____	12.  _____
13.  _____	14. _____	15.  _____	16.  _____

toy	chew	towel	screw
growl	soil	news	royal
boil	point	blouse	tower
cloud	mouth	cowboy	jewel

Beginning blends, digraphs, and silent consonants   Unit 1

The first sounds you hear in words are called the **beginning sounds**. Some beginning sounds are made up of more than one letter. They have special names.

Blends use the sound of each letter close together. Examples: str, gl, fr, sc	Digraphs make a whole new sound. Examples: ch, wh, th, sh	Silent consonants begin with a silent letter. Examples: wr, kn

Find a word from the Word Bank that begins with the same sound as each picture. Write the word on the package.

Word Bank:
skyscraper
whirl
glare
clever
chipmunk
knight
floor
through

1.

2.

3.

4.

5.

6.

7.

8.

Name

Ending blends and digraphs   Unit 1

You may also find blends and digraphs at the ends of words. They are then called **ending sounds**.

Below are vowels with some common ending sounds. Use them to create words on the pyramids. Can you fill in all of the blanks without repeating a word?

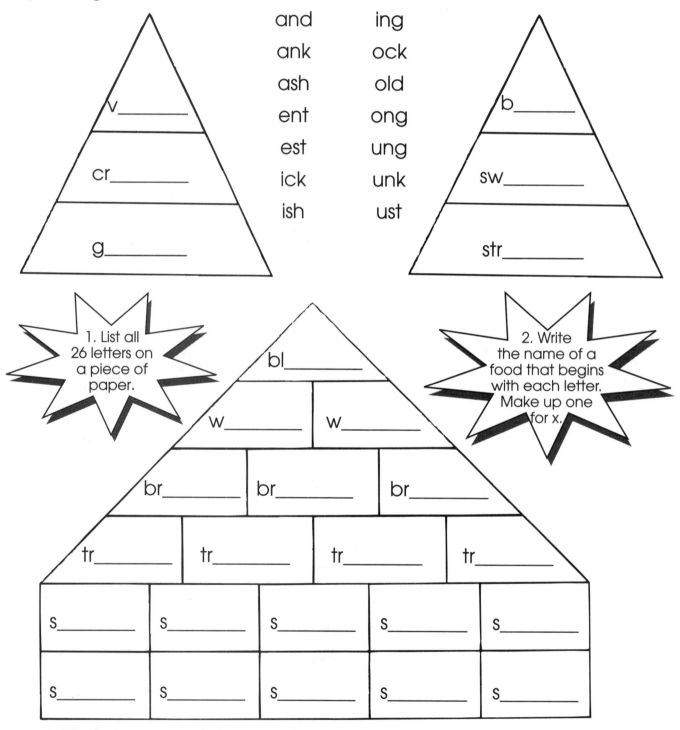

and	ing
ank	ock
ash	old
ent	ong
est	ung
ick	unk
ish	ust

v_____

cr_____

g_____

b_____

sw_____

str_____

1. List all 26 letters on a piece of paper.

2. Write the name of a food that begins with each letter. Make up one for x.

bl_____

w_____   w_____

br_____   br_____   br_____

tr_____   tr_____   tr_____   tr_____

s_____ s_____ s_____ s_____ s_____

s_____ s_____ s_____ s_____ s_____

Name

Read or listen to the directions. Fill in the circle beside the best answer.

❏ Example:

Which word ends with the same sound as **wrong**?

Whisper the sounds you are making to yourself.

write   sung   throne   crown

Ⓐ   Ⓑ   Ⓒ   Ⓓ

Answer: B because sung also ends in <u>ng</u>.

Now try these. You have 20 minutes. Continue until you see ⬡STOP .

Mark the picture with the same sound as the underlined letters in 1–4.

1. n<u>ai</u>l

Ⓐ   Ⓑ   Ⓒ   Ⓓ

2. bi<u>r</u>ch

           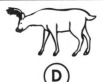

Ⓐ   Ⓑ   Ⓒ   Ⓓ

3. <u>thr</u>ow

20

Ⓐ   Ⓑ   Ⓒ   Ⓓ

4. bla<u>nk</u>

Ⓐ   Ⓑ   Ⓒ   Ⓓ

GO ON ➡

Mark the letters that will complete each word in 5–10.

5.

cl_____

(A) aw   (B) ar

(C) ah   (D) ai

6.

t_____st

(A) oi   (B) oo

(C) oa   (D) oe

7.

sh_____k

(A) er   (B) or

(C) ir   (D) ar

8.

c_____ns

(A) oi   (B) ow

(C) oa   (D) oo

9.

_____are

(A) sc   (B) squ

(C) skw   (D) scu

10.

dr_____

(A) ink   (B) een

(C) ing   (D) enk

GO ON

Unit 1 Test

Mark the word with the same sound as the underlined letters in 11–16.

11. teacher

crank	bread	leap	shell
Ⓐ	Ⓑ	Ⓒ	Ⓓ

12. broom

hood	slope	month	rule
Ⓐ	Ⓑ	Ⓒ	Ⓓ

13. couch

gown	moist	slowly	whole
Ⓐ	Ⓑ	Ⓒ	Ⓓ

14. clang

chase	crown	cheap	clever
Ⓐ	Ⓑ	Ⓒ	Ⓓ

15. string

twig	tangy	stir	thing
Ⓐ	Ⓑ	Ⓒ	Ⓓ

16. hard

chirp	hair	start	happy
Ⓐ	Ⓑ	Ⓒ	Ⓓ

GO ON ➡

Name _____

17. Which word begins with the same sound as **strange**?

slave
(A)

stripe
(B)

sang
(C)

sting
(D)

18. Which word has the same vowel sound as **coast**?

count
(A)

chomp
(B)

hopeful
(C)

towel
(D)

19. Which word ends with the same sound as **spend**?

happened
(A)

tent
(B)

spine
(C)

listen
(D)

20. Which word has the same vowel sound as **write**?

pinned
(A)

sting
(B)

frighten
(C)

wait
(D)

Write three words that have a vowel followed by the letter r.
Each word must be at least four letters long.

1. _____

2. _____

3. _____

STOP

Name

Synonyms

Synonyms are words that have the same or almost the same meaning.

Examples: nice   surprised   huge

                   kind   shocked   enormous

Use the clues to find the matching synonyms to finish the puzzle. Use the words in the Word Bank to help you.

Word Bank: bundle, clean, shine, hardly, smart, middle, lift, forward, new, start

Across

2. wise

5. barely

6. tidy

7. raise

9. fresh

10. begin

Down

1. package

3. center

4. sparkle

8. ahead

Name

Antonyms

Antonyms are words that have opposite meanings.

Examples: sharp   good   many
              dull   evil   few

Find the antonym for each underlined word in the Word Bank. Write its letter on the eraser of the pencil.

A. save   D. careless   G. enemy

B. late   E. serious   H. bright

C. full   F. simple   I. small

1. Be <u>careful</u> climbing trees.

2. The theater lights were <u>dim</u>.

3. Should we <u>spend</u> all of our money?

4. Mrs. Brown's math test was <u>difficult</u>.

5. I'm so <u>hungry</u> I could eat a horse.

6. She left school <u>early</u> to see the dentist.

7. Can my <u>friend</u> come over today, Mom?

8. The <u>playful</u> kittens hid under the couch.

9. The mother kangaroo has a <u>large</u> pouch.

Name

Multiple meaning words

Many of the words we use have more than one meaning. We know which meaning makes sense by reading the rest of the sentence.

Use the Word Bank to find a word that makes sense in both sentences.

step	jam	spring	kind	leaves	log	feet	light

1. As the days grow warmer, we know _____ is coming.

   We watched the rabbit _____ into the hollow log.

2. This piece of wood is three _____ long.

   The concrete is burning my bare _____.

3. I tried to _____ my papers into the backpack.

   She eats grape _____ on her toast.

4. My teacher _____ school after the buses have gone.

   We watched the colorful _____ fall to the ground.

5. The sun's _____ warms our planet Earth.

   The empty bag felt _____ and was easy to carry.

6. _____ over the puddles so your feet stay dry.

   The cat sat on the top _____ all day.

7. What _____ of fish is that?

   A _____ person makes a good friend.

8. We write in a reading _____ each day.

   The frog jumped off the _____ into the water.

Name

Using context clues

Have you ever come to a word that you can sound out, but you do not know what it means? One way to find out its meaning is to use all of the other words to figure out what would make sense. This is called using **context clues**. Using the rest of the sentence will give you clues about the unknown word's meaning.

Look at the pictures of the moon. Use the context clues from each sentence to label the pictures using the underlined words.

1. Look at the <u>full moon</u> tonight. It looks like a giant ball of light.

2. We used flashlights to take our nighttime walk. It was so dark with the <u>new moon</u>.

3. As the tiny sliver of the <u>crescent moon</u> came out, so did the fireflies.

4. Sometimes we can see a <u>half moon</u> during the day. It is funny to see the moon and the sun at the same time.

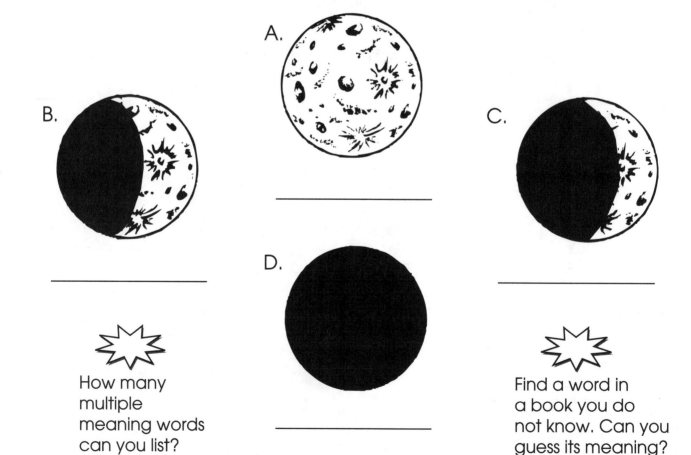

A.

_____

B.

_____

C.

_____

D.

_____

How many multiple meaning words can you list?

Find a word in a book you do not know. Can you guess its meaning?

Name

Using context clues

Sometimes the context clues along with your own ideas will help you make a good guess at a word's meaning.

Use the context clues to make the best choice for each underlined word's meaning.

1. The blue paint turned a <u>pale</u> color when I added water to it.

   bright ○   light ○   green ○

2. Dad cut his hand on the <u>blade</u> of the lawnmower.

   tool for cutting ○   handle ○   wheel ○

3. Dad likes to relax on the <u>sofa</u> after he takes us swimming.

   bike ○   couch ○   stairs ○

4. Would you like a large or small <u>slice</u> of watermelon?

   plate ○   piece ○   picnic ○

5. Prairie dogs sit on <u>mounds</u> to help them see danger coming.

   their tails ○   small hills ○   chairs ○

6. The aquarium has many <u>rare</u> fish that would be hard to see anywhere else.

   special ○   large ○   scary ○

7. The cowboy tried to <u>calm</u> the horses after the loud thunder ended.

   settle down ○   move ○   saddle ○

Name

Analyzing words through analogies

Unit 2

Analogies are one way to compare and analyze words. The best way to solve an analogy is to look only at the first two words. How are they related to one another? Now apply that same relationship to the next set of words.

Example: Finger is to hand as toe is to ____. A finger is part of a hand. What is a toe a part of? The answer is a foot.

Who will win the game of tic-tac-toe? Finish each analogy using a word from the puzzle. Then mark an **X** or **O** over the words on the board to find the winner.

1. Book is to shelf as milk is to _____. Mark X.

2. Three is to triangle as four is to _____. Mark O.

3. Green is to grass as blue is to _____. Mark X.

4. Fly is to spider as hay is to _____. Mark O.

5. Win is to lose as dark is to _____. Mark X.

6. Teacher is to chalk as firefighter is to _____. Mark O.

7. Baseball is to field as swim is to _____. Mark X.

8. Sleep is to bed as eat is to _____. Mark O.

hose	table	square
sky	horse	refrigerator
light	car	pool

Applying analogies   Unit 2

Remember to look for a relationship between the first set of words, then apply the same relationship to the second set.

Complete each analogy using a word from the Word Bank. Then find the answers in the puzzle. They may be written across, down, or diagonally.

Word Bank
hand
temperature
woods
yard
hospital
house
desert
chicken
right
pull

1. Water is to ocean as grass is to _____.

2. Milk is to cow as egg is to _____.

3. Africa is to Earth as kitchen is to _____.

4. Teacher is to school as doctor is to _____.

5. Frog is to pond as camel is to _____.

6. Coral is to ocean as ivy is to _____.

7. Question is to answer as push is to _____.

8. Middle is to center as correct is to _____.

9. Slide is to playground as finger is to _____.

10. Clock is to time as thermometer is to _____.

H	E	B	T	E	I	O	L	T	Y	Z	D	I	O	D
P	O	W	I	T	E	M	P	E	R	A	T	U	R	E
R	A	S	D	L	R	T	U	G	X	E	R	N	H	S
I	Y	N	P	S	F	U	L	C	W	O	O	D	S	E
G	A	D	H	I	K	Q	L	A	M	G	P	O	C	R
H	M	E	C	R	T	L	C	H	I	C	K	E	N	T
T	S	R	J	D	U	A	S	V	N	U	N	O	U	A
Y	H	O	U	S	E	M	L	K	H	I	A	G	W	P

Name

Read or listen to the directions. Fill in the circle beside the best answer.

❑ Example:

What is the opposite of **sweet**?

(A) cake   (B) sour

(C) good   (D) chocolate

Answer: B

If you are unsure, try each answer in the blank.

Now try these. You have 20 minutes. Continue until you see .

---

1. Mark the word that means the same as the underlined word.
   <u>Complete</u> your work.

mark	finish	find	check
(A)	(B)	(C)	(D)

---

2. Mark the word that means the opposite of the underlined word.
   My grandma has an <u>antique</u> dresser from when she was a girl.

big	broken	white	new
(A)	(B)	(C)	(D)

---

3. Mark the sentence in which the underlined word has the same meaning as the underlined word in the sentence below.
   The mall is on the <u>right</u> side of the street.

(A) Do you think that is the <u>right</u> answer?

(B) Clean up your room <u>right</u> away.

(C) Watch for the tigers on the <u>right</u> side of the train.

(D) Is this the <u>right</u> way to tie my shoes?

Name _____

Unit 2 Test

Page 2

---

4. Choose the word that has different meanings but makes sense in both sentences.

Wow! Look at the car _____ after Dad washed it.

The sun will _____ on the plant and help it grow.

now (A) clean (B) shine (C) rise (D)

Mark the word that makes sense in each sentence.

You may want to _____ the Arch in St. Louis. Its _____ is 620 feet.
(5)   (6)

5. (A) build (B) visit | **6.** (A) height (B) color

(C) clean (D) wash | (C) name (D) age

---

7. Cat is to whiskers as elephant is to _____.

trunk (A) big (B) zoo (C) gray (D)

---

8. Protect means _____.

just right (A) to be on time (B) to act nice (C) to keep safe (D)

---

9. Choose the word that has different meanings but makes sense in both sentences.

We came to a _____ in the road.

My baby brother is learning to eat with a _____.

turn (A) fork (B) bump (C) spoon (D)

GO ON

© Carson-Dellosa CD-4316   25   Teach & Test Reading: Grade 2

10. Choose the word that means the opposite of **clear**.

cold	clean	cloudy	wavy
Ⓐ	Ⓑ	Ⓒ	Ⓓ

11. Plane is to sky as boat is to _____.

water	float	ski	swim
Ⓐ	Ⓑ	Ⓒ	Ⓓ

12. Choose the picture that matches the underlined word.

Do not forget to water the <u>fern</u> while Mom is gone.

Ⓐ   Ⓑ   Ⓒ   Ⓓ

13. The opposite of tight is _____.

knot	right	show	loose
Ⓐ	Ⓑ	Ⓒ	Ⓓ

14. Mark the sentence in which the underlined word has the same meaning as the underlined word in the sentence below.

The campers took a break in the <u>shade</u>.

Ⓐ Your shirt is a nice <u>shade</u> of green.

Ⓑ <u>Shade</u> in your picture with chalk.

Ⓒ Pull the <u>shade</u> closed at night.

Ⓓ Let's have a picnic in the <u>shade</u>.

15. Sink is to float as always is to _____.

sometimes	today	never	tomorrow
Ⓐ	Ⓑ	Ⓒ	Ⓓ

GO ON

Unit 2 Test

16. Choose the word that has different meanings but makes sense in both sentences.

The store will _____ early because it is a holiday.
Be sure to _____ the door so bugs do not get in the house.

close (A)   open (B)   sell (C)   spray (D)

Mark the word that makes sense in each sentence.

Last night we ate at my favorite _____. The _____ brought us our food. It was great!   (17)   (18)

17. (A) dinner
(B) restaurant
(C) plate
(D) spaghetti

18. (A) server
(B) table
(C) menu
(D) French fries

---

19. Chair is to sit as bed is to _____.

teddy bear (A)   sleep (B)   jump (C)   pillow (D)

---

20. Can we eat? I am starving. Starving means _____.

lunch (A)   full (B)   food (C)   hungry (D)

Think of a word that has two meanings. Write a sentence for each meaning and underline the word in each.

1. _____

2. _____

STOP

Name

Using a title page

The first page inside the cover of a book is usually a **title page**. It shows the title of the book, the author's name, the publisher, and sometimes gives the copyright date.

title ——→ **Hamsters**
by A. Molengraft ——— author
illustrator ——→ Illustrated by J. D. Maye
copyright date ——→ Miller-Wyne Co. ©2001 ——— publisher

Design a title page for your favorite book below. Be sure to include the title, author, illustrator, publisher, and copyright date. Because these are all special names, they should be capitalized.

Using a table of contents   Unit 3

Most chapter books and longer informational books have a **table of contents** page after the title page. This helps you find parts of the book more quickly.

Your teacher has asked you to write a report about animals. In the report, you must answer all of the questions listed below. It would take you a very long time to read the entire book, so you decide to use the table of contents to help you. Write the chapter and page number where you would begin looking to answer each question.

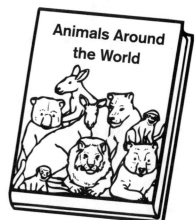

Animals Around the World

Table of Contents

Chapter 1   Mammals (Animals with Fur) 1
Chapter 2   Reptiles (Snakes, Turtles, Alligators)........13
Chapter 3   Amphibians (Frogs and Toads) 21
Chapter 4   Fish 35
Chapter 5   Insects and Spiders 49
Chapter 6   Birds 57

	Chapter to look in	Page to begin looking
1. How long do lions live?		
2. How fast do sailfish swim?		
3. What do snakes eat?		
4. How long does it take for robin eggs to hatch?		
5. Do spiders bite?		
6. Where do poison dart frogs live?		
7. What do beavers eat?		
8. How long do turtles live?		

Name

Using entry words

Unit 3

A dictionary is a book full of words and their meanings. The word you look up is called the **entry word** and its meaning is called a definition.

Use the definitions below to label each picture with its matching entry word.

angle — place where two lines meet

parallel — two lines that never cross

perpendicular — two lines that cross to make a "+"

point — a dot

ray — a point with a line that goes only one way

segment — two points with a line between them

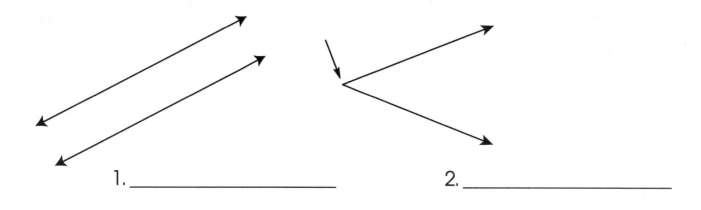

1. _____

2. _____

3. _____

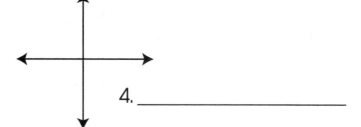

4. _____

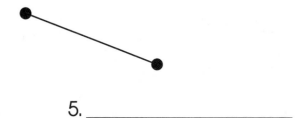

5. _____

6. _____

Using a dictionary   Unit 3

A **dictionary** will give you definitions for nearly all words. To make it easier to find a particular word, the entire dictionary is written in alphabetical order.

The words below belong in a dictionary. Write them in alphabetical order.

might	evening	boil
carp	magnet	icicle

1. _____   4. _____

2. _____   5. _____

3. _____   6. _____

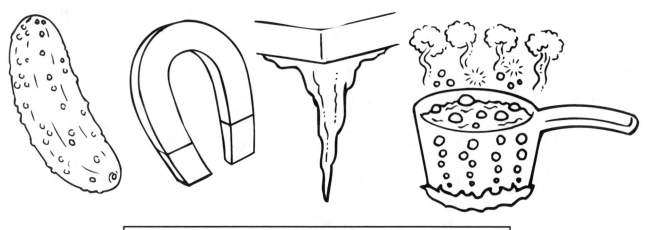

height	pickle	diet
drain	frisky	practice

1. _____   4. _____

2. _____   5. _____

3. _____   6. _____

Name

Maps can help you find your way around different places. They can also help you picture the settings of a story or follow your way through a story. Look for the map key which describes the meaning of each symbol. Also, look for the compass rose which shows direction.

Do you know the story *The Wizard of Oz*? This map shows different settings from the story. Some of the symbols are missing from the map. Use the directions below to finish the map and then answer the questions about the land of Oz.

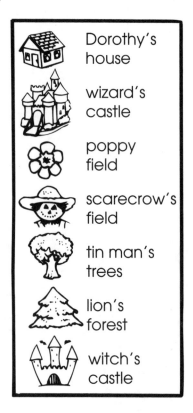

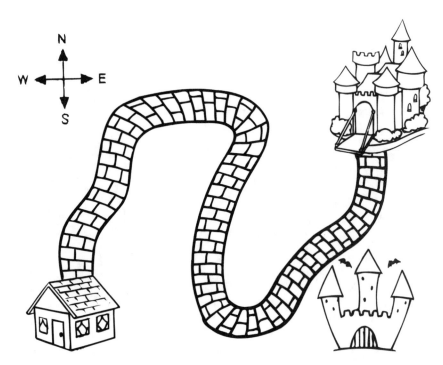

1. Starting at Dorothy's house, follow the yellow brick road north. Draw the scarecrow's field.

2. Continue on the road to the east. Draw the tin man's trees.

3. Follow the road south and draw the lion's forest.

4. Stay on the road past the witch's castle and head north. Draw the poppy field.

What is just south of the wizard's castle? _____

Which direction is Dorothy's house from the scarecrow's field? _____

Name _____

Reading a chart

Charts and **tables** are helpful in organizing information. To read a chart, match the given information from the top and side to find new information in the boxes.

Example: Who will use the science center on Friday?

Look at the chart below. Find the science center along the side and follow it to Friday. You will find Kendra's name in the box.

Centers	Monday	Tuesday	Wednesday	Thursday	Friday
Reading	Sandie	Elena	Sam	Kendra	Evan
Listening	Elena	Sam	Kendra	Evan	Sandie
Math	Sam	Kendra	Evan	Sandie	Elena
Art	Kendra	Evan	Sandie	Elena	Sam
Science	Evan	Sandie	Elena	Sam	Kendra

Use the information from the chart to find the answers.

1. Who will use the art center on Thursday? _____

2. What center will Sam use on Monday? _____

3. On what day will Evan use the science center? _____

4. What center will Sandie use on Friday? _____

5. Who will use the reading center on Wednesday? _____

6. On what day will Elena use the math center? _____

7. On what day will Kendra use the art center? _____

8. What center will Evan use on Thursday? _____

9. Who will use the science center on Thursday? _____

Name

Understanding the main idea

The **main idea** of a story tells what the whole story is about. It does not tell one part of the story or recall one fact from the story. It is the overview for the entire story or paragraph. Titles often tell you something about the main idea.

Example: Which title describes the story below? *The Buck's Antlers*   *A Deer Family*

My family lives near the woods, and we love to watch for deer in our yard. The largest is a male, called a buck. One winter day, we saw the buck had lost its antlers! My teacher told me this is normal. All bucks loose their antlers in the winter and grow new ones in the spring!

The best title is *The Buck's Antlers* because it tells about the whole story. *A Deer Family* does not tell the main idea because the story never mentions the other members of the buck's family.

The titles below describe the main ideas for the stories on page 35. Cut them out and glue them at the top of their partner story. Remember to ask yourself, "Does this title tell about the whole story?"

Caring for Hsing	**The Panda Keeper**
Becoming a Zookeeper	**What Hsing Eats**

Name

See directions on page 34.

1. Brenda Morgan is a zookeeper in Washington, D.C. Brenda has the very important job of caring for a panda named Hsing at the zoo. She has come to know Hsing as a mother knows her child.	2. Brenda has always wanted to work closely with animals and help care for them. As a child, Brenda wanted to be a horse when she grew up! Since she could not become a horse, she became a zookeeper instead.
3. Part of Brenda's job is to watch Hsing closely to be sure he is feeling well. Once, he had an eye infection, and Hsing went blind for a few days. Brenda knew to call the vet for medicine, and now Hsing is well again.	4. Hsing eats many kinds of foods. He likes gruel, which is made of rice, honey, and cheese. He also enjoys apples and bamboo. Brenda thinks his favorite food is carrots.

Creating a title

The **title** of a picture or story should describe the main idea.

The pictures below are from four stories. Study each group of pictures carefully to create a title that describes the main idea. Write the title in front of the pictures.

Title: _____ _____ _____			
Title: _____ _____ _____			
Title: _____ _____ _____			
Title: _____ _____ _____			

Choosing main ideas   Unit 3

Longer stories may be written in paragraphs, each telling about something different. In this case, the title should be about the entire story and each paragraph will have its own main idea that describes the entire paragraph, not the entire story.

Circle a title to describe the story below. Then circle a main idea to describe each paragraph.

Chemicals are everywhere. They make up our air, our houses, our food, and even our bodies. Chemicals help make things different from one another. They make an apple sweet and a lemon sour. They make leaves green.

When the chemicals mix to form something new, it is called a reaction. As a banana ripens, it turns from green to yellow. This is from chemicals changing. When you mix chocolate with milk, you are watching chemicals change, in a tasty way!

1. A good title for this story would be:

   A. Chemicals in Our Bodies

   B. Chemicals Are Tasty

   C. Chemicals Around Us

2. Paragraph 1 is mostly about:

   A. Apples are sweet.

   B. Chemicals are everywhere.

   C. Leaves are green.

3. Paragraph 2 is mostly about:

   A. Chemicals can change.

   B. Bananas turn from green to yellow.

   C. Chocolate milk is tasty.

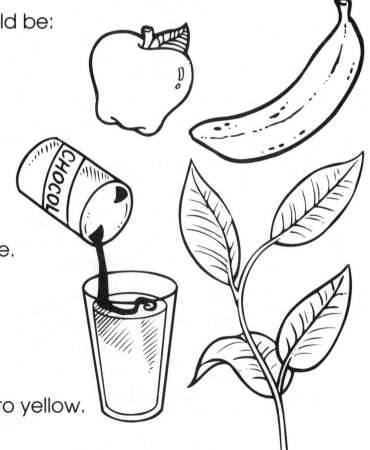

Name

Read or listen to the directions. Fill in the circle beside the best answer.

❏ Example:

The name of the book is called the _____.

(A) title   (B) illustrator

(C) author   (D) publisher

Read all the choices before you answer.

Answer: A because the title is the name of the book.

Now try these. You have 20 minutes. Continue until you see (STOP) .

Name the parts of the title page.

1. (A) title   (B) illustrator
   (C) author   (D) publisher

2. (A) title   (B) illustrator
   (C) author   (D) publisher

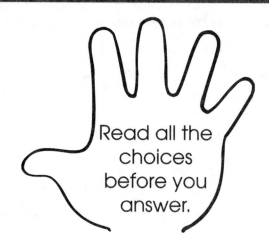

AFRICA

by Peter Hans   (1)

Illustrated by
Kaye Redding

CFW Co.   (2)
©1998

Use the table of contents to answer questions 3–6.

Table of Contents

Chapter 1   Washington as a Boy 3
Chapter 2   Washington as a General 27
Chapter 3   Washington as a President......43
Chapter 4   Remembering Washington 58

3. Which chapter will help you learn about George Washington as president of the U.S.?

(A) 1   (B) 2
(C) 3   (D) 4

GO ON

4. If you begin reading on page 27, you will learn about:

- Ⓐ Washington leading in wars
- Ⓑ Washington's birthday
- Ⓒ Washington getting married
- Ⓓ Washington growing up

5. On which page would you begin reading to learn about Washington's childhood?

- Ⓐ 3
- Ⓑ 27
- Ⓒ 43
- Ⓓ 58

6. What would be the best title for this book?

- Ⓐ The Presidents
- Ⓑ The Life of George Washington
- Ⓒ Washington, D.C.
- Ⓓ George and Martha Washington

Use the map to answer questions 7 and 8.

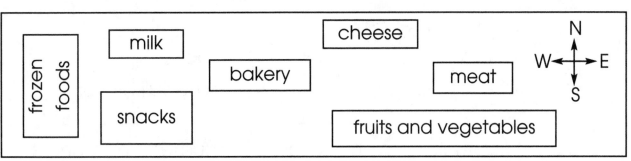

7. What is north of the bakery?

- Ⓐ meat and cheese
- Ⓑ milk and cheese
- Ⓒ milk and snacks
- Ⓓ fruits and vegetables

8. Which direction are the frozen foods from the snacks?

north	south	east	west
Ⓐ	Ⓑ	Ⓒ	Ⓓ

GO ON

Unit 3 Test

Use this part of a dictionary to answer questions 9–11.

mend—to heal	tragic—sad
pastime—a hobby	wrench—a tool used to tighten a bolt
stalk—a large stem	

9. Where would you find a stalk growing?

at the mall (A)   in a bathroom (B)   on TV (C)   in a cornfield (D)

10. How do you spell the word that means sad?

gratic (A)   tragic (B)   cragit (C)   tagric (D)

11. Who would use a wrench?

(A) a nurse   (B) a cook

(C) a repair person   (D) a baseball player

stork   petunia   hammer   bushel   candle

12. If these words were found in a dictionary, which would be first on the page?

stork (A)   candle (B)   bushel (C)   hammer (D)

13. Which word would be last on the page?

stork (A)   candle (B)   bushel (C)   hammer (D)

GO ON

Unit 3 Test

Use the paragraph below to answer questions 14 and 15.

Do not forget to brush your teeth! The foods you eat will mix with the saliva in your mouth to make plaque. If the plaque stays on your teeth too long, it will make your teeth rot. That is why dentists think it is important to brush your teeth two times every day. Do you agree?

14. What is the main idea?

(A) Dentists are smart.

(B) Sometimes we forget to brush our teeth.

(C) Some foods are bad for your teeth.

(D) We should brush our teeth twice a day.

15. Which of these would not make a good title?

(A) No More Plaque!

(B) My Lost Tooth

(C) Brush Away

(D) Keep Your Teeth Clean

Use the chore chart below to answer questions 16 and 17.

	Make bed	Clean room	Pick up toys	Do dishes	Do homework
Mick	√			√	√
Annie	√	√	√		

16. Which job did both children do?

(A) made their beds

(B) cleaned their rooms

(C) picked up toys

(D) did their homework

17. Which jobs did Annie do, but Mick did not do?

(A) dishes and homework

(B) dishes and toys

(C) toys and clean room

(D) homework and clean room

GO ON

Use the information below to answer questions 18–20.

Trees can be placed into two groups: evergreen and deciduous. Evergreen trees stay green throughout the cold winter. Their leaves are often like needles. Christmas trees are evergreens.

Deciduous trees lose their leaves in the fall and grow new ones in the spring. They may have flowers or fruit that grow on them. The trees that turn red, orange, and yellow in the fall are deciduous.

18. Which of these would make a good title for the story?

(A) Christmas Trees   (B) Trees With Needles

(C) The Changing Leaves   (D) Two Types of Trees

19. Paragraph 1 is mostly about:

(A) winter   (B) evergreen trees

(C) deciduous trees   (D) fruit

20. Paragraph 2 is mostly about:

(A) evergreen trees   (B) fall

(C) deciduous trees   (D) fruit

Use a dictionary to find a word that begins with the letter B and is the first entry word on the page. Write your word and its meaning.

_____

_____

_____

Name

Recognizing details   Unit 4

Recognizing details means being able to find specific answers to questions about a story.

A Tasty Butterfly

Butterflies are lovely to look at, but here is how to make one you can eat!

You will need:

    2 frozen pancakes
    1 banana
    2 grapes
    2 pieces of link sausage
    jelly or jam
    2 toothpicks

Here is how to make it:

- Toast the pancakes and cut them in half. This will make four pieces because butterflies have four wings.

- Peel the banana and place it on a plate. This will be the butterfly's body.

- Spread jelly or jam on the "wings."

- Use the toothpicks to hold the grapes on the banana as eyes.

- Cook the sausage and place it at the top of the banana as antennae.

Use details from the story to fill in the missing words.

1. The _____ will make the butterfly's body.

2. The wings will be covered with _____.

3. Butterflies have four _____.

4. The antennae will be made from _____.

5. A butterfly has two _____ to see with.

Name

Using pictures to show sequence

Sequencing means putting events from a story in the order they happened.

Unit 4

Number the pictures 1–6 to show the order of the steps to make a tasty butterfly. Use the recipe on page 43 to help you.

Using visual discrimination with details

Some details are harder to find because they are hidden as descriptive words (adjectives and adverbs). When you are reading for details, pay close attention to the describing words.

On Our Way to Camp

Crystal waved good-bye to her parents and threw her striped backpack over her shoulder. She found her best friend, Sarah, on the bus and sat down next to her. "Camp is going to be so much fun," Sarah said, "but I think I will miss my family."

Crystal unzipped her backpack. "Maybe a candy bar will help you feel better," she said.

The girls giggled and finished their snack in no time. They watched out the window as busy highways became small roads and buildings became lakes. "This really makes me feel funny," Sarah said as she slumped down.

"I have cards in the pocket of my backpack. Should we play?" Crystal asked.

"Okay," answered Sarah. She beat Crystal twice. By the time they had started their third game, Sarah had forgotten all about missing her family.

Use details from the story to figure out which backpack below belongs to Crystal. Circle it. You may want to reread the story, watching for details about the backpack.

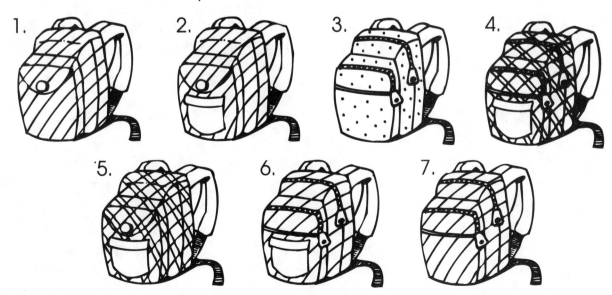

Name

numbering sentences to sequence events

To sequence a story, use a few important parts of the story written as sentences. Your job will be to read each sentence and remember the sequence. If you are unsure, reread the story, paying close attention to the parts that are scrambled.

Read the important parts below from the story "On Our Way to Camp" on page 45. Then number them in order 1–7.

☐ Sarah told Crystal that she will miss her family.

☐ Sarah felt better about missing her family.

☐ The girls shared a candy bar.

☐ Crystal told her parents good-bye and jumped on the bus.

☐ Crystal and Sarah noticed they were leaving the city and heading toward camp.

☐ Crystal found Sarah on the bus.

☐ Sarah beat Crystal twice at cards.

Choose seven events from a story to tell an adult. Be sure to tell them in order.

Name

Using details to answer questions   Unit 4

To use details to answer questions about a story, you will need to pay close attention as you read and go back to the story if you are unsure.

No Broken Friendship

Matthew and Brandon have been best friends since kindergarten. One day when Brandon was playing at Matthew's house, he jumped from the swing set and landed in a strange way. "My arm," he shouted. One look at Brandon's arm told Matthew that it was broken.

Brandon's parents took him to the hospital where the doctor x-rayed his arm. The doctor put a blue cast on him and told Brandon that his bones would grow back in place. He also reminded Brandon not to take any risks, like falling or playing too rough, during the next eight weeks.

The next day, Brandon took his X ray to school and told the class his story. They had many questions, and Brandon answered them as best he could. Matthew asked, "Do you want to play tic-tac-toe instead of wall ball at recess today?"

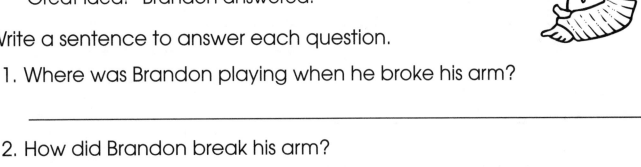

"Great idea!" Brandon answered.

Write a sentence to answer each question.

1. Where was Brandon playing when he broke his arm?

_____

2. How did Brandon break his arm?

_____

3. Who took Brandon to the hospital?

_____

4. How did the doctor know Brandon's arm was broken?

_____

5. What will the boys do at recess?

_____

Name

Sequencing with key words   Unit 4

Sequencing a story will help you retell the story to others. **Key words** are often used to
give you clues about the sequence of a story's events. Words like first, next, then, and
last are examples of such words.

Choose four important parts of the story "No Broken Friendship" on
page 47. Finish each sentence and draw a picture to match. Be sure
to use the correct sequence.

1. First, _____

_____

_____

2. Then _____

_____

_____

3. Next, _____

_____

_____

4. Last, _____

_____

_____

Using context to find details

Sometimes the details you are looking for are words you have never seen before. Remember to use the context of the sentence to help you learn about the new word.

A Sunny Flower

The sunflower starts as a seed and begins to grow a strong taproot. Soon the green stalk begins to grow toward the warmth of the sun. As the plant grows, it forms a bud that will some day become a flower. The plant faces the east as the sun rises in the morning. Then it follows the sun across the sky until it is facing west when the sun sets. As the flower's bud blooms, it unfolds into large golden petals. The center of the flower is full of seeds. The seeds are either eaten or planted so more sunny flowers can grow!

Use details from the story to complete the puzzle. If you are unsure of a word's meaning, use the story's context clues to help you. You must use correct spelling for the puzzle to work.

Across

1. A sunflower grows toward the _____.

2. Seeds grow in the ___ of the flower.

3. Sunflowers have large golden _____.

4. The plant forms a _____ that will become a flower.

6. The _____ begins to grow from the seed into the soil.

Down

1. The _____ can be called a sunny flower.

4. The bud _____ into a flower.

5. The _____ is like a stem.

Sequencing with a diagram

Sometimes the sequence of an event is more interesting with illustrations. This type of picture is called a **diagram** because it helps us visually understand information.

Read the story "A Sunny Flower" on page 49. Cut out the pictures at the bottom of the page. Glue them in sequence to show the life cycle of a sunflower.

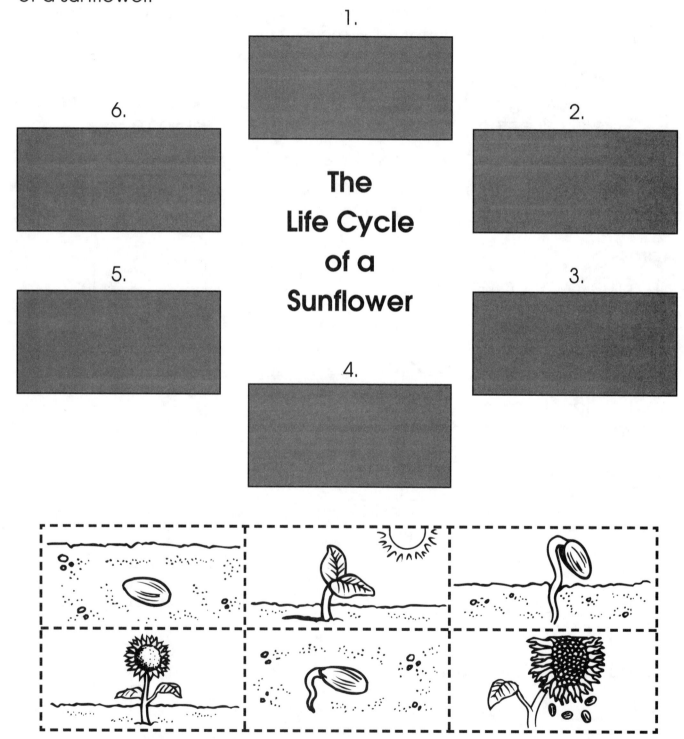

1.

6.

2.

**The
Life Cycle
of a
Sunflower**

5.

3.

4.

50

Name

Read or listen to the directions. Fill in the circle beside the best answer.

❏ Example:

Mitch has a new pet, a lizard. His name is Dino because Mitch thinks he looks like a dinosaur. Dino sleeps in a glass cage with a light to keep him warm.

Why does Dino sleep with a light?

(A) Dino is afraid of the dark.

(B) Dino looks like a dinosaur.

(C) Dino's cage is glass.

(D) Dino needs to stay warm.

When you are unsure, go back and read the story again.

Answer: D because the story says the light keeps him warm.

Now try these. You have 25 minutes. Continue until you see ⬡STOP .

Read the story to help you answer questions 1–3.

Last week, Anna took care of her friend's pet turtle. It was more work than Anna thought. She had to cut up carrots, lettuce, and broccoli for him to eat. When she let him out of his cage to walk around in the grass, she had to check on him all the time. Her last job was to make sure that the turtle had lots of water. Anna liked her job, but she was tired.

1. What did Anna feed the turtle?

(A) She fed him large carrots.

(B) She fed him lettuce and apples.

(C) She fed him broccoli, lettuce, and carrots.

(D) She fed him lettuce, broccoli, and fruit.

GO ON

Name

2. Why did Anna let the turtle out of his cage?

    (A) to let him eat   (B) to let him walk around

    (C) to let him get water   (D) to let him find lettuce

3. What was the last part of Anna's job?

    (A) to let him walk in the grass   (B) to let him eat

    (C) to cut up carrots and broccoli   (D) to check his water

Read the story to help you answer questions 4–10.

    Lilly knew today was important. Her big brother was coming home from college for summer vacation. First, she helped her mom clean his room. Then she set his favorite movies out where he could find them. Next, Lilly put some of her brother's favorite soda in the refrigerator to get cold. Last, she sat on the step and waited.

For questions 4–7, put the sentences below in order as they happened in the story.

    A. Lilly put some soda in the refrigerator.

    B. She waited on the step for her brother.

    C. She set out her brother's favorite movies.

    D. Lilly helped clean her brother's room.

4. First,

(A) (B)
(C) (D)

5. Then

(A) (B)
(C) (D)

6. Next,

(A) (B)
(C) (D)

7. Last,

(A) (B)
(C) (D)

GO ON

8. Why is Lilly being so helpful?

(A) Her sister is coming home from college today.

(B) Her mom is coming home from a trip today.

(C) She likes cleaning her brother's room.

(D) Her brother is coming home today.

9. Why is Lilly sitting on the steps?

(A) Her brother will be home soon.

(B) Her best friend is coming to play.

(C) She is watching for the mail carrier.

(D) She is looking for her dog.

10. Why is Lilly's brother coming home?

(A) It is Christmas vacation.

(B) He is done with college.

(C) It is summer vacation.

(D) He is coming over for dinner.

GO ON

Name

Unit 4 Test

Page 4

Read the paragraphs to answer questions 11–17.

Hurricanes are huge storms that begin at sea. Warm air from the ocean rises toward the sky. Then cool air begins swirling around the warm air. As water from the ocean is lifted into the air, a storm begins to form. Soon, huge thunderclouds begin to drop rain in heavy sheets. The storm spins like a top across the water and may even reach land. The hurricane will not die until it passes over cooler water or crosses land.

Hurricanes have different names in other parts of the world. They are called cyclones in the Indian Ocean. When this storm forms in the western Pacific Ocean, it is called a typhoon. In the Atlantic Ocean and the eastern North Pacific Ocean, they are called hurricanes. No matter what the name, they are huge, spinning storms.

For questions 11–14, put the sentences below in order to tell how a hurricane is formed.

A. Warm air rises toward the sky.

B. Huge sheets of rain drop from thunderclouds.

C. Cool air swirls around the warm air.

D. The storm spins like a top across the ocean.

11. First,
(A) (B)
(C) (D)

12. Then
(A) (B)
(C) (D)

13. Next,
(A) (B)
(C) (D)

14. Last,
(A) (B)
(C) (D)

15. Where do hurricanes begin?

(A) in the sky   (B) at sea

(C) over land   (D) other parts of the world

GO ON

16. A typhoon is a storm in the _____.

    (A) western Pacific Ocean   (B) Atlantic Ocean

    (C) Indian Ocean   (D) North Sea

17. Which is not the name for these spinning storms?

    (A) typhoon   (B) hurricane

    (C) tornado   (D) cyclone

Read the letter to help you answer questions 18–20.

Dear Frankie,

    Vacation has been great so far. Yesterday we went to a wax museum. There were lots of statues of famous people and they are all carved out of wax! My mom liked the one of Pocahontas and my dad liked Johnny Appleseed, but my favorite was George Washington. He was wearing real clothes and he even had on a wig. He looked so real I thought he might talk. And then he did! The museum had a speaker hooked to the statue in the back, so they could make him talk. It was so cool! Next time, maybe your family can come with us!

                  Your pal,

                  Kevin

18. Who went to the wax museum?

    (A) Frankie   (B) George Washington

    (C) Kevin   (D) Kevin and his family

19. Who was Kevin's favorite statue?

    (A) Johnny Appleseed   (B) George Washington

    (C) Pocahontas   (D) the president

GO ON

20. How did the statue talk?

(A) There was a man standing behind him.

(B) Kevin made him talk.

(C) There was a speaker behind him.

(D) He was alive.

Write about four parts of your school day on the lines below. Be sure to use the correct order.

First, _____

_____

Then, _____

_____

Next, _____

_____

Last, _____

_____

Name

Read or listen to the directions. Fill in the circle beside the best answer.

 Example:

Mark the picture with the same sound as the underlined letter.

m<u>a</u>ple

 (A)

 (B)

(C)

(D)

Remember your Helping Hand Strategies:

 1. Whisper the sounds you are making to yourself.

 2. If you are unsure, try each answer in the blank.

 3. Read all the choices before you answer.

 4. When you are unsure, go back and read the story again.

Answer: B, because cave also has a long a sound.

Now try these. You have 25 minutes. Continue until you see ⬡STOP .

---

1. Mark the letters that will complete the word.

j_____n

ar
(A)

er
(B)

ou
(C)

oi
(D)

---

2. Mark the word with the same sound as the underlined letters.

gr<u>ow</u>th

clown
(A)

ground
(B)

hope
(C)

gown
(D)

 GO ON

3. Petal is to flower as tire is to _____.

car
(A)

race
(B)

wheel
(C)

road
(D)

4. Choose the word that has different meanings but makes sense in both sentences.

Our family is taking a _____ to Florida.
Be careful not to _____ on those branches.

vacation
(A)

trip
(B)

step
(C)

fall
(D)

Use the table of contents to answer questions 5 and 6.

China

5. Which chapter will help you learn where pandas live?

(A) Chapter 1
(B) Chapter 2
(C) Chapter 3
(D) Chapter 4

6. If you begin reading on page 47, you might learn about:

(A) How to use chopsticks when you are eating.

(B) What your name looks like in Chinese.

(C) How to dress like a Chinese girl or boy.

(D) How to celebrate Chinese New Year.

GO ON

Read the steps to help you answer questions 7–9.

1. Get a long piece of yarn.
2. Put a bead 2 inches from the bottom of the yarn.
3. Tie the string in a knot around the bead.
4. Slip 12 more beads on the string to make a pattern.
5. Put on the largest bead.
6. Slip 12 more beads on the string to match the pattern.
7. Tie the loose end of the string to the bead at the other end.
8. Make another knot.
9. Put the necklace around your neck and show it to a friend.

7. Choose the best title.

(A) Yarn and Beads

(B) Making a Knot

(C) How to Make a Bead Necklace

(D) Wearing a Necklace

8. How many pieces of yarn will you need to make the necklace.

1
(A)

12
(B)

2
(C)

4
(D)

9. What should you do before you slip 12 more beads on to match the pattern?

(A) Make another knot.

(B) Put on the largest bead.

(C) Put a bead 2 inches from the bottom of the yarn.

(D) Tie the loose end of the string to the bead at the other end.

GO ON

Midway Review Test

tweezers	dinosaur	porcupine
pencil	baton	

10. If these entry words were found in a dictionary, which would be first?

pencil
(A)

porcupine
(B)

baton
(C)

dinosaur
(D)

11. Which two words are most likely to be on the same page of the dictionary?

(A) baton and dinosaur

(B) dinosaur and pencil

(C) porcupine and tweezers

(D) pencil and porcupine

12. Which word has the same vowel sound as **brook**?

football
(A)

because
(B)

claw
(C)

dinosaur
(D)

13. Choose the word that means the opposite of **smooth**.

soft
(A)

rough
(B)

fluffy
(C)

slippery
(D)

14. What does the illustrator do for a book?

(A) writes the story

(B) puts the book together

(C) names the book

(D) draws the pictures

15. Which word begins with the same sound as **chance**?

climb
(A)

chump
(B)

clap
(C)

shake
(D)

GO ON

Midway Review Test

Read the story to help you answer questions 16 and 17.

Lexy's dad was having a birthday. She wanted to give him some golf balls, so she had been saving her money. She still needed another five dollars. Lexy had an idea. She asked her mom if she could water the flowers to earn extra money. Her mom agreed to pay her three dollars for her work. Then Lexy asked if she could earn another two dollars taking out the trash. Her mother agreed again. After finishing both jobs, Lexy rushed to the store. She wrapped the gift and handed it to her dad. She knew this was the perfect gift!

16. What job did Lexy offer to do for two dollars?

(A) Go shopping for her dad's present.

(B) Water the flowers.

(C) Take out the trash.

(D) Play golf with her dad.

17. If the boxes below show the order in which the story happened, what is missing in box 5?

4	5	6
Lexy finished her jobs.		Lexy wrapped the balls.

(A) Lexy wanted to give her dad golf balls for his birthday.

(B) Lexy had saved her money.

(C) Lexy asked if she could water the flowers.

(D) Lexy went to the store to buy golf balls.

Name

18. Mark the letters that will complete the word.

sw_____

and	ing	unk	est
Ⓐ	Ⓑ	Ⓒ	Ⓓ

19. Mark the sentence in which the underlined word has the same meaning as the underlined word in the sentence below.

My mother asked me to give my teacher a <u>note</u>.

Ⓐ Dorothy's song has a high <u>note</u> at the end.

Ⓑ Did you <u>note</u> the phone number?

Ⓒ I will write a thank-you <u>note</u> to Aunt Bev.

Ⓓ I had to learn the name of the <u>notes</u> before I could play them.

20. Mark the meaning of the underlined word.

My dog has learned to <u>obey</u> me when I tell him to stay.

Ⓐ listen to   Ⓑ play with

Ⓒ run away from   Ⓓ jump on

Write the title of a story you know well. Then write a sentence telling the story's main idea.

Title: _____

Main Idea: _____

_____

Analyzing a character's actions

Unit 5

Characters are the people, animals, or animated objects that are found in a story. They seem to be brought to life by their actions and they may even "grow up" or change as people do in real life.

A Real King

Larry the Lion had been king of the grasslands for a very long time, but the animals felt they needed a new king. Larry had become lazy, mean, and selfish. When Larry learned of this, he set the animals free and laughed to himself, "They will beg to have me back!" But the animals did not beg to have Larry back, and so he moved away.

One lonely day, Larry found a mouse that was balancing on a branch in the river. He helped the mouse to the shore. Later, Larry found a baby zebra who was lost from his mother. Larry was kind and helped the little zebra find his home.

When the animals learned of Larry's kind acts, they asked him to become their king again. They needed a helpful and strong king, which Larry now seemed to be. Larry the Lion had become a real king!

Did you notice that Larry's character changed as the story continued? Complete the lists below by writing three words to describe Larry at the beginning of the story and three words to describe Larry at the end of the story.

King Larry at the Beginning

1. _____
2. _____
3. _____

King Larry at the End

1. _____
2. _____
3. _____

63

Name

Analyzing a character's emotions   Unit 5

To make stories more interesting, characters often face issues that can be good or bad, just as you do. The character will show his feelings by what he says or does.

Each of these children are feeling a certain way. Read each sign for clues. Then use the words from the Word Bank to finish the signs. Be sure to draw faces on the children to show their feelings.

scared

proud

worried

disappointed

excited

1. I really worked hard and spelled every word the right way on my test. I feel _____.

2. I watched a movie about ghosts last night. Now I feel _____.

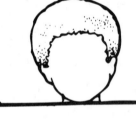

3. I forgot my backpack on the bus. I'm _____ about getting it back.

4. I'm so _____ that it rained on the day of my big game.

5. I'm so _____ to see that funny new movie.

Name

Comparing characters

Stories with more than one important character can be fun to read because the characters are usually different from one another, just as the people you know are different.

City Mouse, Country Mouse

Once upon a time, a city mouse went to visit her friend in the country. The country mouse had spent the day gathering grain and dried pieces of corn in order to greet her friend with a nice meal. The city mouse was surprised to find her poor friend living in a cold tree stump and eating such scraps. So, she invited the country mouse to visit her in the city. The country mouse agreed.

The country mouse could not believe her eyes when she arrived! Her friend lived in a warm hole behind the fireplace of a large home. She was even more surprised to find all of the fine foods that were left behind after a party the night before. The country mouse wished that she could live in the city as well.

Suddenly, the family's cat ran in and chased the two mice away. He nearly caught the country mouse with his sharp claws. As the friends raced back to the mouse hole, the country mouse said, "I'm sorry, friend, but I would rather live a simple life eating corn and grain than live a fancy life in fear!" The country mouse went back home.

The two characters in this story are different from one another. Mark an X in each box to describe the correct mouse.

	City Mouse	Country Mouse
1. She feasted daily on fine foods.		
2. She would rather have a simple, safe life.		
3. She gathered grain and corn.		
4. She lived in a large house.		
5. She was surprised by all of the fine foods.		
6. She lived in a warm place.		

Discovering the setting

The **setting** is the place where a story takes place. The story usually has clues about the time of year or the time in history. In the story "City Mouse, Country Mouse" on page 65, the two settings told us more about the characters and helped us picture the story in our minds.

Do you know which mouse is the country mouse and which is the city mouse in the pictures below? Without a setting it is hard to tell. Draw the background settings with clues that will let the reader tell them apart.

Name _____

Stories are more interesting when a character has to face a problem and figure out a way to solve it. In "The Wizard of Oz," Dorothy faces the problem of getting back home. The story would be far less exciting if she did not have to ask the wizard for help.

Write a sentence describing the problems in each rhyme. Write another sentence telling how the characters solve the problem.

Humpty Dumpty sat on a wall.

Humpty Dumpty had a great fall.

All the king's horses and all the king's men

Couldn't put Humpty together again.

The first problem is _____

_____

The second problem is _____

How might the problem be solved? _____

_____

Jack and Jill went up the hill
To fetch a pail of water.
Jack fell down and broke his crown
And Jill came tumbling after.

The first problem is _____

The second problem is _____

How might the problem be solved? _____

_____

Discovering a plot   Unit 5

As characters try to solve their problems, a story develops and other things begin to happen. This is called the **plot** of the story. In "The Wizard of Oz," Dorothy meets three good friends and faces a wicked witch as part of the plot. The plot is often divided into three parts: the beginning, middle, and end.

The pictures below tell three stories. Label the beginning, middle, and end of each.

1.

   _____   _____   _____

2.

   _____   _____   _____

3.

   _____   _____   _____

Name

Developing a story

We have learned about the characters, setting, problem, and plot of a story. They are called the story's elements. Now let's put it all together!

Follow each step below and on page 70 to plan a story on your own.

1. Plan two characters. Write their names and three words to describe them.

   #1 _____

          1. _____

          2. _____

          3. _____

   #2 _____

          1. _____

          2. _____

          3. _____

2. Where will your story take place? Write about your setting.

   _____

   _____

3. What problem will your characters face?

   _____

   _____

4. How will they solve it?

   _____

   _____

5. How will your plot unfold? Plan the beginning, middle, and end of your story.

6. Turn your plan into a story or book! Use paper and pencil or a computer. Share your story with a friend.

Name

Read or listen to the directions. Fill in the circle beside the best answer.

❑ Example:

Jose rushed through the door and handed his mother his math test. She screamed and threw him into the air.

How do you think Jose did on his math test?

(A) okay   (B) great

(C) poorly   (D) awful

More than one answer may seem correct! Be sure to compare the choices.

Answer: B because Jose probably did a great job since his mother was excited.

Now try these. You have 25 minutes. Continue until you see ⬡STOP.

Use these story parts to show what is being described in 1–4.

   A. the way to solve the problem

   B. the setting

   C. the characters

   D. the problem

1. Sissy and Spotty are Persian cats. They have long, fluffy hair.

(A)   (B)   (C)   (D)

2. The two cats lived with their owner in a large city. Their house was beautiful, and the cats had everything they could ever want, except excitement.

(A)   (B)   (C)   (D)

GO ON

---

3. The cats had always wanted to see the city. So they set off on their own. It was not long before they met a growling dog that began to chase them.

     Ⓐ   Ⓑ   Ⓒ   Ⓓ

4. The cats climbed a chimney, leaving the dog behind. From the top, they could see the whole city. This was just what they had always wanted.

     Ⓐ   Ⓑ   Ⓒ   Ⓓ

Read the story to answer questions 5–9.

There once lived a poor Chinese boy name Ma Lien. He worked hard in the rice fields, dreaming of the one day he would become a painter. But Ma Lien did not even have a paintbrush. Instead, he used rocks to scratch on stones or drew pictures with his fingers in the wet sand.

One night as Ma Lien lay in bed, he dreamed that he had a special paintbrush. Whatever he painted with it came to life!

Ma Lien used his special brush to help people. He painted roosters for poor families in his village and toys for children.

A greedy king heard about the special paintbrush. He ordered Ma Lien to paint a mountain of gold for him. Ma Lien painted a gold mountain surrounded by a huge sea. The king ordered him to paint a ship so the king could sail to the mountain. As the king and his men stepped on the ship, Ma Lien painted stormy clouds that sunk the king's ship.

Ma Lien woke up and went to the rice fields to work. Eventually he did acquire a paintbrush. Though it wasn't a "special" paintbrush, what he painted was special. He remembered the dream and always used his talent wisely.

5. Which of these does not describe Ma Lien?

(A) He lived in China.　　(B) He was selfish.

(C) He helped people.　　(D) He wanted to become
　　　　　　　　　　　　　　　　a painter.

6. The king acted in a _____ way.

　　brave　　　　helpful　　　　selfish　　　　kind
　　(A)　　　　　(B)　　　　　(C)　　　　　(D)

7. How were the king and Ma Lien the same?

(A) They both dreamed of a paintbrush.

(B) They both worked in the rice fields.

(C) They both wanted to help people.

(D) They both lived in China.

8. Who was the most important character(s) in this story?

　　the king　　　Ma Lien　　the king's men　　the rooster
　　(A)　　　　　(B)　　　　　(C)　　　　　(D)

9. Which problem was solved in Ma Lien's dream?

(A) Ma Lien was poor.

(B) The king was greedy.

(C) The king's ship was sunk.

(D) The work in the fields was finished.

GO ON ▷

Unit 5 Test

Read the story to answer questions 10–15.

Tommy was tired of the way Aaron and his friends acted at school. They were always taking the ball away from him at recess and breaking his pencils at the writing center. His mom told him to forget about it, but Tommy could not. He had a better idea.

He brought a package to school with Aaron's name on it. Aaron was confused. "What is this?" he asked.

"Just open it," Tommy replied.

Inside Aaron found a ball with his name on it and a package of pencils. "Now we can both be happy," Tommy said. Aaron smiled.

10. How would you describe Aaron at the beginning of the story?

mean	nice	friendly	funny
Ⓐ	Ⓑ	Ⓒ	Ⓓ

11. How are Aaron and Tommy alike?

Ⓐ They are not friendly.

Ⓑ They go to the same school.

Ⓒ They like to break pencils.

Ⓓ They solve problems wisely.

12. How do you think Tommy feels at the end of the story?

Ⓐ happy to get back at Aaron

Ⓑ mad that Aaron was mean to him

Ⓒ proud to come up with an answer to his problem

Ⓓ selfish because he wants the ball back

13. What was the biggest problem in the story?

(A) Tommy's mom did not help him.

(B) Tommy did not like recess.

(C) Aaron did not have any pencils.

(D) Aaron and his friends were mean.

14. What is the setting for the story?

(A) school

(B) Tommy's house

(C) Aaron's house

(D) the store

15. Which part of the plot happened in the middle of the story?

(A) Aaron smiled at Tommy.

(B) Aaron took Tommy's ball.

(C) Tommy had an idea.

(D) Tommy was tired of the way Aaron acted.

16. Which of these words would not be used to describe a character's feelings?

unhappy	angry	excited	cowboy
(A)	(B)	(C)	(D)

17. Which is not a story element?

characters	paper	setting	plot
(A)	(B)	(C)	(D)

GO ON

75

Read the story to answer questions 18–20.

There was once a group of mice who had decided to solve the problem of the cat chasing them. Young Mouse said, "Let's put a bell around the cat's neck. Then we will always hear him coming." The other mice stood and clapped their hands. They put Young Mouse up on their shoulders because they thought it was such a good idea!

Then Old Mouse stood and asked, "Which one of you will put the bell around the cat's neck?" The other mice looked at one another. They put Young Mouse down and began to think of a new idea.

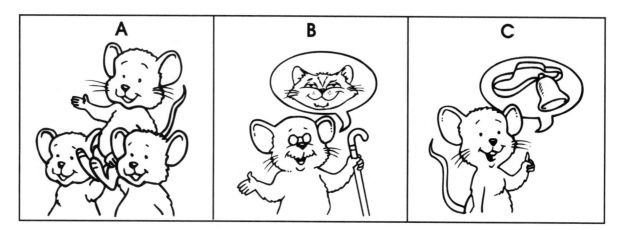

18. Which picture shows the beginning of the story? (A) (B) (C)

19. Which picture shows the middle of the story? (A) (B) (C)

20. Which picture shows the end of the story? (A) (B) (C)

Write four words that could be used to describe a setting.

1. _____   2. _____

3. _____   4. _____

Name

Cause and effect

Many stories add a **cause** and **effect** to help you understand why something has happened in the story. Let's think about the story "Little Red Riding Hood."

<u>Effect</u> (what happened)—Little Red Riding Hood thought her grandma looked strange.

<u>Cause</u> (what made it happen)—It was really the wolf dressed up!

Read the effects below. Find the cause for each and write the matching letter in the blank.

Effect	**Cause**
_____ 1. The animals ran to hide.	A. The snowstorm lasted for two days.
_____ 2. Two pigs ran to their brother's house.	B. Jack planted the magic beans.
_____ 3. Schools were closed last Thursday and Friday.	C. They heard the hunter's footsteps.
_____ 4. Tara's dog jumped out of the tub.	D. Someone had broken its chair.
_____ 5. The little bear was upset.	E. The wolf had blown their houses down.
_____ 6. A huge beanstalk grew toward the sky.	F. It did not like getting a bath.

Name

Creating causes   Unit 6

There are a number of effects that can happen after the cause. These effects can make a story happy, sad, scary, or funny.

Write an ending for each story. You will be writing the cause!

What a morning! I was sound asleep in my bed when I heard my mother open the garage door to take out the trash. The next thing I knew, my mom was screaming and calling my name! I ran downstairs and found my mom standing on a chair holding a broom.

_____

_____

_____

_____

Lunch was pretty exciting at school today. I was sitting across from Leslie. She was talking about her trip to the mountains when she suddenly looked down at her plate and screamed!

_____

_____

_____

_____

Name

Recording cause and effect

In the book <u>Alexander and the Terrible, Horrible, No Good, Very Bad Day</u> by Judith Viorst (Simon & Schuster Children's, 1976), a young boy feels like everything has gone wrong. Think about the causes for his bad day as you read this summary of the book.

<u>Alexander and the Terrible, Horrible, No Good, Very Bad Day</u>

Alexander was having a bad day. Before he even ate breakfast, he discovered gum in his hair, tripped over his skateboard, and dropped his sweater in the sink full of water. At school that day, Alexander's teacher seemed to like Paul's picture of a boat more than Alexander's invisible picture. And later his teacher asked him to practice counting because he left out a number. Alexander was having a bad day. When he went to pick up his dad from work, Alexander made a mess by playing with the copy machine even though he was told not to. By the time Alexander went to bed, he was sure it had been a very bad day.

Have you ever had a day like Alexander's? Have you ever had the opposite type of day when everything goes just right? Think about what caused you to have a good or bad day. Then make a list of the effects and their causes.

My _____ Day
(Great, Horrible)

First, _____
(What happened?)

because _____.
(What made it happen?)

Then, _____
(What happened?)

because _____.
(What made it happen?)

Last, _____
(What happened?)

because_____.
(What made it happen?)

Name

Determining causes   Unit 6

Alexander's day seemed pretty bad because of all the effects (bad things that happened), but there is a cause (what made the bad things happen) for each of them. Recognizing the causes can help solve problems in the future.

Help Alexander have a better day next time by telling him the causes for his bad day.

Dear Alexander,

Sorry to hear about your bad day, but I think you may have caused some of it. Next time remember:

1. Don't _____,
then you won't have gum in your hair.

2. Be sure to _____,
then you won't trip over your skateboard.

3. At school you should always _____.
I'm sure your teacher would have liked your picture if you had drawn one.

4. The next time you go to your dad's office you should not

_____,

then your dad won't be angry.

I hope these ideas help. Cheer up! Tomorrow will be a better day!

Your pal,

Three dogs show up at your house. What caused this?

_____

Locating similarities and differences

Unit 6

Part of reading carefully is watching for ways that story elements are alike (**similarities**) and ways that they are different (**differences**). Read this summary of <u>The Rats' Daughter</u> written by Joel Cook (Boyds Mill Press Inc., 1993), watching for similarities and differences.

The Rats' Daughter

Mother and Father Rat were very proud of their daughter, and they wanted her to marry someone very special.

Father Rat chose a fine and noble rat as Daughter Rat's husband, but Mother Rat disagreed. She thought her daughter should marry the sun.

The rats went to visit the sun. The sun told the rats that perhaps the cloud would make a better husband for Daughter Rat.

Then, the three rats went to visit the cloud. The cloud recommended that Daughter Rat marry the powerful wind. It was true, the wind did throw the cloud about.

Now the Rat Family tried to catch the wind to talk. The wind showed them that the wall was stronger because he could block the wind. He thought Daughter Rat should marry the wall.

Mother Rat asked the wall if he would like to marry Daughter Rat, but he answered that there was someone else Daughter Rat should marry instead. The wall said, "Do you see these small holes in me? I cannot stop something from passing through them." The noble rat had made the holes in the wall. The rats watched as the noble rat crawled through a hole.

Father Rat was pleased, because this was the noble rat that he had chosen before. The two were married, and they lived happily ever after.

Label each sentence with **S** if it shows a similarity and **D** if it shows a difference.

 1. The sun, the cloud, the wind, and the wall each sent the rat family to someone else.

 2. The sun felt that the cloud was the strongest. The wind felt that the wall was the strongest.

 3. Father Rat chose a noble rat to marry the daughter. Mother Rat chose the sun.

 4. Mother Rat and Father Rat wanted their daughter to marry someone special.

Name _____

Sometimes stories give you clues that help you form an opinion. This is called **drawing** a **conclusion**. The answers to some questions may or may not be in the story, but by reading carefully, you will have an idea about what the answers might be.

Write a sentence to answer each question using the story on page 81.

1. What pattern do you notice in the story <u>The Rat's Daughter</u>?

_____

_____

_____

2. Were you surprised that the wall thought the noble rat was the best choice? Why?

_____

_____

_____

_____

3. What else could fit through a hole in a wall? How would this have changed the story?

_____

_____

_____

_____

Name

Researching for similarities and differences
Drawing conclusions based on research

Unit 6

When you read to find information, similarities and differences can help you learn more.

Mammals or Birds?

Bats are amazing animals. They have ears and a nose similar to other furry animals, but they have wings like a bird. Or do they? Scientists have found that a bat's wing bones are like our hands. They have a thumb and four fingers that form their wings. The wings are not covered in feathers, but with a thick skin. Baby bats are born alive and drink milk from their mother. So are they mammals or birds?

To help you decide whether bats are mammal or birds, make a list of similarities and differences below.

Mammals

Alike: _____

_____

_____

_____

Different: _____

_____

_____

_____

Birds

Alike: _____

_____

_____

_____

Different: _____

_____

_____

_____

What have you concluded? Is a bat a bird or mammal? _____

Name _____

Read or listen to the directions. Fill in the circle beside the best answer.

❏ Example:

What may have caused this effect:

Everyone in the park ran for cover!

(A) They heard music.

(B) An airplane flew over.

(C) It began to storm.

(D) They were selling hot dogs.

Read carefully and go back to the story if you are unsure.

Answer: C because a storm would cause people to run for cover.

Now try these. You have 30 minutes. Continue until you see ⬡STOP.

Read the story to answer 1–8.

Paul Bunyan: A Tall Tale

The story of Paul Bunyan begins long ago in the woodlands. When Paul was a baby, he was too big to fit in the house! As he got older, he was so big that his parents had to teach him not to step on houses or farm animals. Back then, people needed lots of trees to build their houses and the railroads. The men who cut down the trees were called loggers. Since Paul was so big, he could swing his ax a few times to cut down a whole forest. He became a great logger.

One winter, Paul was out walking in the snow and found a baby blue ox the size of a small mountain. He named the ox Babe. They became close friends. Babe would carry the wood that Paul cut down. He would also take water to the loggers. Paul strapped a huge tub on Babe's back and filled it with water. Sometimes some would spill out and land in one of Babe's huge footprints. That is why there are so many lakes in Minnesota!

GO ON

Once, Babe tripped and the whole bucket of water spilled. It made the Mississippi River!

As Paul and Babe finished logging in one area, they would move on. One time, Paul started dragging his ax behind him. The ditch it made was so huge that we now call it the Grand Canyon!

No one knows where Paul and Babe are today. Some people believe that they are in Alaska, still cutting down trees. No matter where they are, you can be sure they are leaving their mark!

1. Paul was so big that his parents had to teach him _____.

    (A) not to yell too loud   (B) not to run

    (C) not to step on houses   (D) not to hit other children

2. How were Babe and Paul similar?

    (A) They were both blue.   (B) They were both babies.

    (C) They both helped loggers.   (D) They both carried water.

3. How does this story say the Mississippi River was made?

    (A) Paul dragged his ax behind him.

    (B) Babe spilled a bucket of water.

    (C) The snow melted.

    (D) Paul stepped in the mud.

4. Paul probably named the ox Babe because _____

    (A) he was a baby.   (B) he was so small.

    (C) he looked like a pig.   (D) he cried a lot.

5. What was the effect of Paul dragging his ax behind him?

   (A) The Mississippi River was made.

   (B) Many lakes were made.

   (C) Minnesota was made.

   (D) The Grand Canyon was made.

6. How was life different in the story of Paul Bunyan than it is now?

   (A) People needed water.

   (B) People lived in houses.

   (C) People had farm animals.

   (D) People were building railroads.

7. How was Paul's job different from Babe's?

   (A) One helped the loggers, and one helped the farmers.

   (B) One cut the trees down, and one carried the trees.

   (C) One worked inside, and one worked outside.

   (D) One liked his job, and one did not.

8. Why was Paul such a great logger?

   (A) He could cut down a forest quickly.

   (B) He liked cutting down trees.

   (C) He had an ox.

   (D) He moved to new places all the time.

GO ON

Read the story to answer questions 9–14.

Get Out of My House!

Millions of termites work together to build large dirt mounds in the grassy plains of Africa, Australia, and South America. After their work is done, many other animals come along to use the mounds, each in their own way.

Because the mounds are often the highest part of the land, some animals use them to get a better view. A mother cheetah and her babies climb the mound and stand on top to look for food. The mother then leaves her babies on the mound to watch her hunt. This is how they will learn to hunt for themselves.

Other animals use the mounds to find food. Aardvarks use their sharp claws to dig through the walls of the mounds. Then they stick their long noses through the hole to make a meal of termites.

With a hole through it, a termite mound becomes the perfect home for a mongoose family. They live in groups of 12 to 15 members and work together to watch for enemies. The termite mound makes a great lookout!

Some animals use the mounds for something quite funny . . . to scratch themselves. Elephants and rhinos get itchy skin from bug bites, scratches, and dry mud. They stand near the mounds and rub themselves on them. Sometimes they stand over the mounds to scratch their bellies!

Who would ever think a small bug like a termite could be so important to so many other animals?

9. How does an aardvark use termite mounds?

(A) It gets food from them.

(B) It uses them as a lookout.

(C) It sleeps in them.

(D) It hunts for larger animals on top of them.

GO ON

Unit 6 Test

10. Which does not cause an elephant's skin to itch?

(A) dry mud   (B) scratches

(C) bug bites   (D) chicken pox

11. How do the mongoose and the cheetah use the mounds in a similar way?

(A) They both get food from them.

(B) They both use them as homes.

(C) They both use them to get better views.

(D) They both use them to scratch themselves.

12. In this story, how are termite mounds like a hotel?

(A) They are the same size.

(B) They have food and places to sleep.

(C) They are made of mud.

(D) They can be found in your town.

13. Who builds the mounds?

(A) mongooses   (B) cheetahs

(C) termites   (D) aardvarks

14. Why might a mother cheetah leave her babies alone on the mound?

(A) because they can't walk   (B) because she forgot them

(C) so they can play   (D) so they can watch her hunt

GO ON

Unit 6 Test

Read the story to answer 15–20.

A Day with an Orangutan

Fireball woke up early in the rain forest. He reached out to pull on a leaf, waking his mother. "Come on, Mom," Fireball called out. He grabbed hold of a vine and swung out across the trees, searching for ripe fruit. Suddenly, it began raining. Fireball did not want to get wet, so he held a piece of wood over his head. "Much better," he thought.

When the rain stopped, Fireball spotted some orange fur through the trees. It was his mom. She was holding a vine between her feet and had stretched across to the other vine, which she was holding in her hands. Fireball saw his chance. He jumped onto her belly and began rocking back and forth. "Whee!" he yelled. Then he noticed something in his mother's hand. He pulled her fingers away from her thumb. Inside he found a small piece of fruit.

"You are so curious, Fireball," his mother said. "Let's find something for you to eat." They spent the afternoon searching for more ripe fruit.

Soon, it was getting dark, telling Fireball and his mother that it was time to build this evening's nest. They gathered branches and leaves, making a nest high in the trees. Fireball cuddled next to his mother and fell asleep.

15. Orangutan babies are different from human babies because

(A) they use their hands.   (B) they play with their moms.

(C) they are curious.   (D) they sleep in nests.

16. Which is true about baby orangutans?

(A) They live alone.   (B) They do not like to get wet.

(C) They live in the desert.   (D) They do not like to eat fruit.

17. Fireball used a piece of wood in a similar way that we use _____.

a spoon   an umbrella   a book   a swing
(A)   (B)   (C)   (D)

GO ON

18. Where do you think Fireball got his name?

(A) Orangutans are orange.

(B) There was a fire in the rain forest.

(C) He liked to play with balls.

(D) He did not want to get wet.

19. What caused Fireball's mom to wake up?

(A) Fireball started shouting.

(B) Fireball was swinging on her belly.

(C) Fireball was hungry.

(D) Fireball was pulling on a leaf.

20. What caused Fireball and his mother to start building a nest?

(A) It was getting wet.

(B) Fireball was getting hungry.

(C) Fireball did not want to get wet.

(D) It was getting dark.

Write three ways that your day is similar to Fireball's.

1. _____

2. _____

3. _____

Fact vs. opinion   Unit 7

Facts are real and true pieces of information. **Opinions** are ideas, feelings, or beliefs.

Color the facts green and the opinions blue. $\underline{\underline{OR}}$ - shade in all the facts if you don't have crayons.

1. Baby blue whales gain about 200 pounds per day.

2. Blue whales have no teeth.

3. It would be cool to touch a blue whale.

4. Blue whales are prettier than killer whales.

5. Blue whales are the largest mammals.

6. Blue whales are so big that they are scary.

7. We should have blue whales at the zoo.

Name

Discovering facts and opinions

Informational passages are written to teach you something. In them you may find facts, opinions, or a mix of both.

Gorillas

Gorillas live in the mountains and forests of Zaire, which is in Africa. Because they are peaceful animals, scientists have been lucky enough to study them. They found that gorillas live in groups made up of several females, their babies, and one or more males. A baby gorilla does not live with its mother long enough. After only three years, it sets off on its own. Each evening, gorillas build nests to sleep in by picking leaves and laying down on them. Gorillas eat tasty foods that include fruits, leaves, and juicy stems. Gorillas are becoming extinct because their forests are being destroyed. We should help save their forests and mountains.

Write three facts from the passage.

1. _____

2. _____

3. _____

Write three opinions from the passage.

1. _____

2. _____

3. _____

Name

Classifying by time

Classifying means putting things into groups. One way to make groups is by days, months, or years. Your photo album may be classified by time.

Classify your day into three groups: morning, afternoon, and evening. Write three activities that belong in each group.

My Morning

1. _____

2. _____

3. _____

My Afternoon

1. _____

2. _____

3. _____

My Evening

1. _____

2. _____

3. _____

Classifying by similarities

Unit 7

Another way to classify is to look for similarities and differences.

Read the passage. Cut out the birds below. Classify them by the shapes of their beaks and glue them on page 95.

Bird Beaks

Though they have wings and lay eggs, birds are not all the same. By looking closely at a bird's beak, you can learn much about it.

- A large, sharp, curved beak tells you that the bird is a meat-eater. The hooked shape of the beak helps the bird tear skin from its prey before eating it.

- Birds with straight, sharp beaks often feed on insects and worms. They will also dig into the ground looking for worms or caterpillars.

- Birds with short, curved beaks are seed-eating birds. The short beak is strong enough to crack through the tough outer shells of seeds and nuts.

- A few birds have long, thin beaks that are used to suck nectar from flowers.

94

Name

Meat-Eating Birds	Worm- and Insect-Eating Birds

Seed-Eating Birds	Nectar-Sucking Birds

Name

Classifying by characteristics

When you are looking for the thing that does not belong in the group, try to find the one thing the others have in common. Example: ball, bike, scooter, pencil (The pencil does not fit with the others because it is used for writing. All the others are used for playing.)

Cross out the word that does not belong with the others.

1. apple banana potato watermelon	2. whale bobcat squirrel raccoon	3. boat car airplane road	4. boots hat mittens snowman
5. towel soap shampoo shoes	6. cotton rock pillow feather	7. candle flashlight mirror lantern	8. bitter sour lemon sweet
9. star moon rocket planet	10. piano drum song guitar	11. maple rose daisy sunflower	12. wagon sled scooter bike

Go to the park. Make
a list of 15 things you see there.
Then divide the list into three groups.
Give each group a name.

Predicting the outcome using pictures

To **predict** is to use clues from a story to guess what will happen next.

The pictures below tell short stories. Draw a picture to show how you predict each story will end.

Name

Predicting a character   Unit 7

Some stories give you clues about its characters, without ever telling you who they are.

Use the clues in the poem to predict the character. Write the number

Who's There?

Who's there? Was that the breeze? Or is something hiding behind those trees? _____

Who's there? I heard a sound. I see eyes that are big and round. _____

Who's there? Come along! I see four legs, big and strong. _____

Who's there? The light is dim, but I don't think that you will swim. _____

Who's there? Did you hear me call? You don't look very small. _____

Who's there? Can you fly? I see a tail going low and high. _____

Who's there? Should I hide from sight? I see whiskers that are long and white. _____

Who's there? Come back! I see something orange and black. _____

One of these characters fits all of the clues in the poem. Circle it.

Predicting outcomes   Unit 7

There are often clues hidden in a story that give you an idea of what will happen next.

Use the clues from the story to predict what happened. Put an **X** by the sentence that tells what probably happened next.

Oh Brother!

My three-year-old brother is crazy! He has such a mind of his own, and he likes to do things he shouldn't! This morning we took him to the park, and I told Mom I would keep an eye on him. On our way there, Zach spotted a flower and wanted to pick it for me. I told him that we should leave the flower for everyone to enjoy. As soon as I turned around _____.

_____ Zach gave me a hug.

_____ Zach asked me to swing with him.

_____ Zach picked the flower.

I chased Zach to the playground. He wanted to slide down the big slide. I told him to wait until I said "Go" so I could catch him at the bottom. I ducked under the slide to get ready. Suddenly I heard Zach laughing. I looked up, and _____.

_____ I saw Zach coming down the slide.

_____ I saw a blue jay fly by.

_____ I saw kids tickling Zach.

Soon, it was time for lunch. Mom brought sandwiches, chips, and lemonade. Zach found some cookies in the basket, too. I asked him not to eat all of them because I wanted one for the ride home. Later, as we jumped in the car, I reached for a cookie. I should have known that _____.

_____ Zach had fallen asleep.

_____ Zach had muddy shoes.

_____ Zach had eaten all of the cookies.

Name

Read or listen to the directions. Fill in the circle beside the best answer.

❑ Example:

Read the story. What will happen next?

Billy put on his coat and hat. He heard his mom honk the horn of the car.

(A) Billy read a book about cars.

(B) Billy will eat breakfast

(C) Billy will call a friend.

(D) Billy will jump in the car.

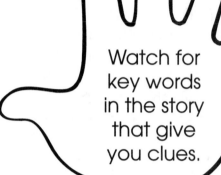

Watch for key words in the story that give you clues.

Answer: D because Billy's mom must be waiting for him to leave.

Now try these. You have 25 minutes. Continue until you see ⬡STOP .

---

1. Mark the sentence that is a fact.

(A) Plants need water.

(B) Plants are pretty.

(C) Everyone should have a plant.

(D) Ferns are the easiest plants to grow.

---

2. Mark the sentence that is an opinion.

(A) There are seven colors in the rainbow.

(B) Rainbows are made when the sun shines through the rain.

(C) Rainbows are the best!

(D) Sometimes two rainbows can form on top of one another.

GO ON

3. Which picture does not belong in the group?

 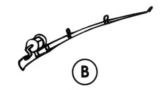  

(A)   (B)   (C)   (D)

4. David packed his bag. He put a toothbrush, pajamas, and a book inside. Where will David go?

(A) to school   (B) to the store

(C) to the pool   (D) to his grandma's

Read the letter to help you answer questions 5–8.

Dear Aunt Lisa,

    The kids at my school are selling wrapping paper to earn money for new computers. We have 20 computers now, but we would like to get more. The kids who sell the most paper will win one of these prizes:

    I am trying to sell $30.00 worth of paper so I will win the movie ticket. It is the best prize. I only need to sell $7.00 more. I know your family has birthdays coming up, so I hope you need some wrapping paper.

Love,

Meg

5. Which of the prizes seems different from the others?

(A)   (B)   (C)   (D)

GO ON

6. Which is an opinion from the letter?

(A) The kids are selling wrapping paper.

(B) The movie ticket is the best prize.

(C) Aunt Lisa's family has birthdays coming soon.

(D) Meg needs to sell $7.00 to win the ticket.

7. What do you think Aunt Lisa will do when she reads the letter?

(A) She will throw it away.

(B) She will go to the movies.

(C) She will order wrapping paper.

(D) She will get a birthday cake.

8. Which is not a fact from the letter?

(A) The school has 20 computers.

(B) The kids who sell the most paper win prizes.

(C) Meg is trying to sell $30.00 in paper.

(D) The kids should try really hard to earn money.

Use the paragraph to answer questions 9 and 10.

Pedro had a part in the school play. He had to wear a green suit. It had a long tail and huge teeth. "Hey," said Pedro's father, "I did not think there were any of you guys left on Earth anymore!"

9. Which animal is Pedro probably dressed as?

a frog	a snake	a dinosaur	a lizard
(A)	(B)	(C)	(D)

GO ON

10. Where do you think Pedro will wear his costume in the story?

(A) at school   (B) at the library

(C) at a Halloween party   (D) on a stage

Use the story to answer questions 11–13.

Jonah was mad! He worked all morning sorting his ocean sticker collection, and now some were missing from the table! Jonah's sister came by wearing a crown colored with markers. At every point there was a sticker!

11. What might Jonah be thinking?

(A) that his sister looks pretty

(B) that his sister took his stickers

(C) that he wants a crown

(D) that his sister is funny

12. Which of these might be one of the missing stickers?

   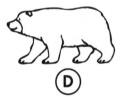

(A)   (B)   (C)   (D)

13. Which of these is not a fact from the story?

(A) Jonah's sister took the stickers.

(B) Jonah's stickers were missing.

(C) Jonah was angry.

(D) Jonah's sister was wearing a crown.

GO ON

When J.J. got home, he found a note that said his mom had gone to the store. She asked him to put his books away and have a small snack, but not candy. She asked him not to play with the stereo and wrote that she would be home by 4:00. She also promised that if things went well, J.J. would earn an extra dollar.

14. What should J.J. do?

(A) call his friends to come over

(B) put his books away

(C) get out the candy

(D) turn on the stereo

15. J.J. will probably do a good job because

(A) he wants some candy.

(B) he likes to listen to the stereo.

(C) he wants to earn an extra dollar.

(D) he likes snacks.

Mark the thing that does not belong in each group in 16–20.

16.	milk (A)	straw (B)	juice (C)	lemonade (D)
17.	setting (A)	library (B)	plot (C)	character (D)
18.	slide (A)	swing (B)	bike (C)	monkey bars (D)

GO ON

19.   window   door   roof   barn
          (A)   (B)   (C)   (D)

20.   butterfly   toad   ladybug   grasshopper
          (A)   (B)   (C)   (D)

Write a fact about your classroom. Write an opinion about your classroom.

Fact: _____

_____

Opinion: _____

_____

Name

Fact vs. fantasy

The events in a story can be divided into two groups: **fact** (real) or **fantasy** (make-believe).

The blocks below tell a story. Read them in order. Then color the parts that are facts yellow and the parts that are fantasy green. The yellow spaces will make a path for the frog to follow.

1. Once upon a time, there was a princess named Anna.	2. One day, Anna lost her favorite ball in the lake.	3. She started to cry. Suddenly, a frog jumped out of the lake.	4. "Hello," he said. "I'll get your ball if you promise to take me home."
5. The princess agreed. The frog jumped in and threw the ball to Anna.	6. "Now I can eat and sleep with you," the frog said.	7. Princess Anna laughed and ran back to the palace without the frog.	8. The frog was angry that Anna had broken her promise.
9. The frog went to the palace and knocked on the door.	10. The frog told the king how Anna had broken her promise.	11. The king said to Anna, "You must always keep your promises."	12. So the frog ate dinner from Anna's plate. "Yummy," he said.
13. Then the frog put on his pajamas and jumped onto Anna's bed.	14. Anna began to cry and the frog suddenly turned into a prince.	15. Anna and the prince were married.	16. Anna had learned to always keep her promises.

Name

Turning facts into fantasy   Unit 8

Writers can turn almost anything into fantasy, which makes the reader use his imagination.

Write the next sentence for each idea, turning it into fantasy.

1. The clock struck midnight.

_____

_____

2. My dog had been playing in the mud!

_____

_____

3. I looked in my desk at school.

_____

_____

4. The girl looked more closely at the butterfly.

_____

_____

Making an evaluation

Unit 8

To **evaluate** means to consider the right and wrong options. In stories, this may mean a character has a decision to make. Will it be the right one?

Use the details from the story to evaluate the characters.

Last One in Is a Rotten Egg!

"Hurray! We get to swim at summer camp today," shouted Logan as he jumped in the back of the car.

"I don't really want to," answered his brother, Nate. Every summer it was the same. Logan would swim away and have fun while Nate sat on the steps of the pool watching.

The boys spotted their friends right away, and one of them shouted, "Last one in is a rotten egg!" Logan turned to Nate. He saw his brother's eyes fill with tears.

1. What do you think Logan should do? _____

_____

2. What do you think Nate should do? _____

_____

Logan called out, "I'm coming!" and jumped in. Nate sat down on the edge of the pool.

He watched as the others jumped off the diving board and chased diving rings. Once, a ring landed by Nate, and Logan came after it. Nate stood up and threw the ring back in the water. "That gives me an idea," said Logan. "You can throw in the rings, and we will dive for them."

3. What do you think will happen next? _____

_____

The boys spent the rest of the afternoon chasing rings as Nate threw them. "Maybe someday you can throw the rings for me," Nate told Logan as they were leaving the pool.

Creating options for evaluations

Unit 8

Given the same situation, a character can make different decisions that will change the story.

Next to each face, write two different ways the story could end, one that is the right decision and one that is the wrong decision.

The Clay Necklace

Miss Jenkin's class spent all afternoon working on projects for Saturday's Native American fair. Lynette and Jeffrey were to make a clay necklace. "I will work on the beads, and you can make the clay sun that will hang in the middle," Lynette told Jeffrey. Lynette carefully shaped beads out of clay and strung them on a piece of yarn. Jeffrey quickly made a ball of clay and smashed it down flat. "I am done," he called and ran outside for recess.

The next day, Lynette was sick and could not come to the fair. Jeffrey's family looked for the necklace he had told them about. There it was. Jeffrey noticed something was different. The clay sun that hung from the middle of the necklace had been carefully carved and painted. It was beautiful!

"There you are, Jeffrey," said Miss Jenkins. "I wanted to tell you how great your work is on the clay sun! You must have spent a lot of time on it."

Name

Following directions using a picture

It is important to read directions one at a time and follow them exactly. Sometimes it is helpful to check them off as you work.

Follow each step in the directions below. Use a check mark to help you follow along.

Mount Kilimanjaro

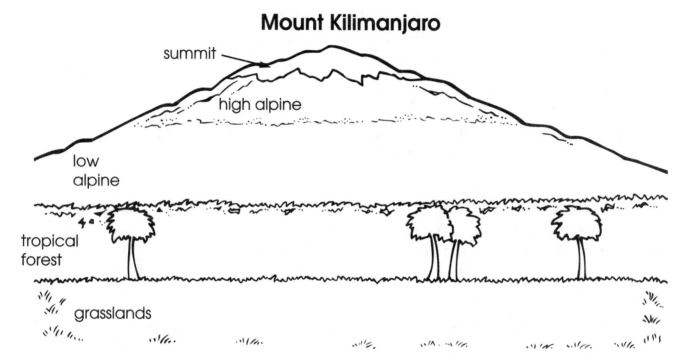

Mount Kilimanjaro is in Africa. The area is grouped into five parts. Different animals are found in four of the parts.

- [ ] Draw a farmer and a bird in the grasslands.
- [ ] Color the grasslands yellow.
- [ ] Draw a monkey, leopard, and lion in the tropical forest.
- [ ] Color the tropical forest dark green.
- [ ] Draw an elephant, buffalo, and eagle in the low alpine.
- [ ] Color the low alpine light green.
- [ ] Draw a spider and an insect in the high alpine.
- [ ] Color the high alpine brown.
- [ ] Color the summit white.

Name

Following directions using a map

Unit 8

Most directions need to be followed in sequence, or they will not make sense. Again, it helps to mark them off as you work, so you will not accidentally skip anything.

Follow the directions in order. Mark them off as you work.

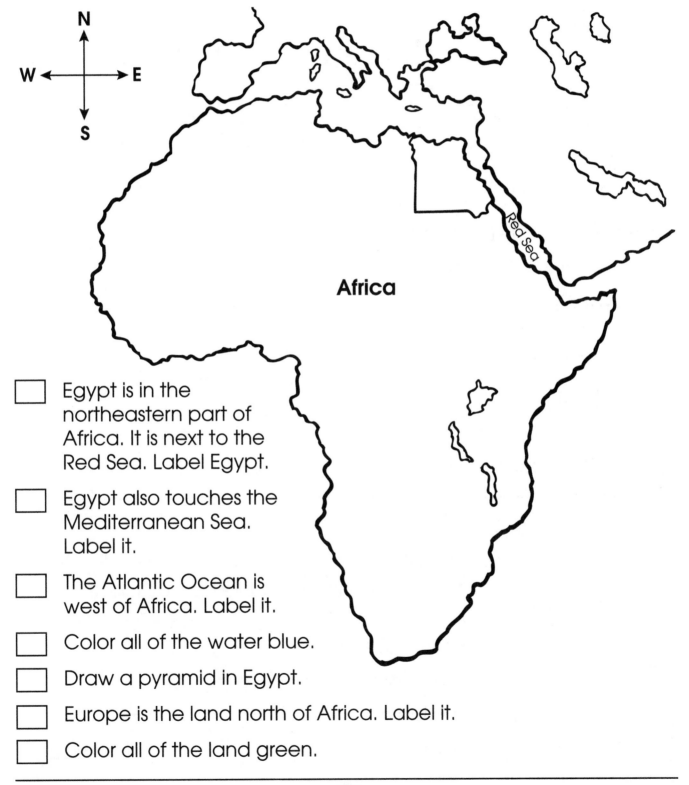

☐ Egypt is in the northeastern part of Africa. It is next to the Red Sea. Label Egypt.

☐ Egypt also touches the Mediterranean Sea. Label it.

☐ The Atlantic Ocean is west of Africa. Label it.

☐ Color all of the water blue.

☐ Draw a pyramid in Egypt.

☐ Europe is the land north of Africa. Label it.

☐ Color all of the land green.

Name

Read or listen to the directions. Fill in the circle for the best answer.

❑ Example:

A make-believe story is called a _____.

(A) fantasy

(B) real

(C) fact

(D) opinion

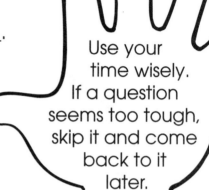

Use your time wisely. If a question seems too tough, skip it and come back to it later.

Answer: A because a fantasy is not real.

Now try these. You have 25 minutes. Continue until you see .

1. Which of these could not really happen?

(A) The cow came into the barn.

(B) The cow sat down in the hay.

(C) A pig came over to the cow.

(D) "Good evening," said the pig.

2. Which of these could really happen?

(A) My cat caught four mice and brought them to our door.

(B) My dog, Sparky, makes my bed while I am at school.

(C) One of my fish can jump out of its bowl, do a flip, and land back in the water.

(D) My rabbit, Snowy, grows carrots in our garden.

3. Which of these is probably the title of a fantasy book?

(A) Snakes and Turtles   (B) The Flying Turtles

(C) Baby Snakes   (D) Frogs and Toads

4. Mark the picture that matches the directions.

Fold your paper in half. Open it again. Write your name at the top.

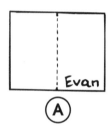
(A)

Deb
(B)

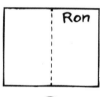
Ron
(C)

Dee
(D)

5. Dana is pretending to be a fantasy animal. Which picture shows the animal Dana is pretending to be?

(A)

(B)

(C)

(D)

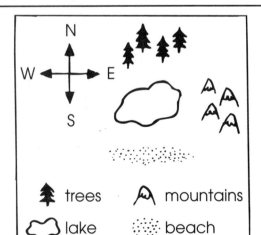

6. Which direction was not followed correctly?

(A) Draw four trees in the north.

(B) Draw mountains in the west.

(C) Draw a beach in the south.

(D) Draw a lake in the center.

GO ON

For questions 7–10, match each picture with its directions.

A.

B.

C.

D.

7. Draw the sun in the sky. Draw an apple tree under the sun. Draw a flower in the corner and a dog near it.

   Ⓐ   Ⓑ   Ⓒ   Ⓓ

8. Draw the sun in the sky. Draw a pine tree. Draw a bird in the tree. Draw a flower in the corner and a dog near it.

   Ⓐ   Ⓑ   Ⓒ   Ⓓ

9. Draw clouds in the sky. Draw a pine tree near the clouds. Draw a flower in the corner and a cat near it.

   Ⓐ   Ⓑ   Ⓒ   Ⓓ

10. Draw clouds in the sky. Draw a tree near the clouds. Draw a bird in the tree. Draw a flower in the corner and a cat near it.

   Ⓐ   Ⓑ   Ⓒ   Ⓓ

11. Which of these is probably the title of a story about facts?

   Ⓐ The Teddy Bear Dance   Ⓑ Our Earth

   Ⓒ The Land of the Dragons   Ⓓ The Purple Cheetah

GO ON ➡

Will had been begging for a puppy, but his parents kept putting it off. They said a puppy would be too much work. Will asked them to think about it, and he promised he would take care of the puppy all by himself.

On Will's tenth birthday, his parents surprised him with a new puppy. He could not believe it! Will named the puppy Frisky and carefully set out his food and water bowls. Then he showed Frisky how to scratch at the back door when he wanted to go out. "That was easy," he thought as he went to bed that night.

12. Why do you think Will's parents decided to get him a puppy?

(A) because it would be easy

(B) because he promised to take care of a puppy

(C) because they loved puppies

(D) because he was cute

13. What should Frisky do when he wants to go out?

(A) cry at the back door   (B) go to his water bowl

(C) scratch at the back door   (D) scratch at Will's bed

Will woke early the next morning to the sound of whining. "What is that?" he asked himself. Then he rolled over and went back to sleep. Soon, Will's mother came to his door. "Will, you need to get up and let Frisky out. He has been waiting for you."

14. What should Will do?

(A) Go back to sleep.   (B) Call his mom to let Frisky out.

(C) Put Frisky in bed with him.   (D) Let Frisky out the back door.

Later that day, Will was watching a movie and eating popcorn with his friend. Just as the best part of the movie started, Frisky scratched at the back door.

15. What should Will do?

(A) Get up and let Frisky out now.

(B) Let Frisky out after the movie.

(C) Eat more popcorn.

(D) Ask his mom to let Frisky out.

After dinner, Will was on his way outside to play ball. He noticed that Frisky's water bowl was empty. He remembered his promise to his parents and picked up the bowl. He knew he was lucky to have a puppy, even with all the work.

16. What should Will do?

(A) Go play ball.   (B) Call his friends.

(C) Fill the water bowl.   (D) Eat dinner.

Max was scared. His parents told him that his new school would be fun, but he already missed his old friends. He walked into the classroom, and a tall boy walked up to him.

17. What should the boy say to Max?

(A) "Move out of my way."   (B) "You look funny."

(C) "Who are you?"   (D) "Hi, my name is Joey."

GO ON

18. Charlie wanted to carry something real for the costume party. Which picture shows something he may carry?

(A)

(B)

(C)

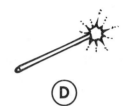
(D)

Carlos and Nick got a little too excited while wrestling in the house. They knocked over a table, and a vase crashed to the floor. They knew Nick's mom would be disappointed. She had asked them to play outside.

19. Which of these is not a good choice for the boys?

(A) Tell Nick's mom.   (B) Offer to pay for the vase.

(C) Keep wrestling.   (D) Tell Nick's mom they are sorry.

20. What did the boys probably learn?

(A) never wrestle again

(B) never get excited again

(C) always wrestle outside

(D) move everything that can break first

Follow the directions below.

1. Draw three cats sitting side by side.

2. Color the one in the middle black.

3. Put a hat on a brown cat.

(STOP)

Final Review Test

Read or listen to the directions. Fill in the circle beside the best answer.

❑ Example:

You must be <u>cautious</u> when crossing the street.

What is the meaning of the underlined word?

(A) friendly

(B) slow

(C) careful

(D) alone

Answer: C because cautious means to be careful.

Now try these.
You have 30 minutes.
Continue until you see ⬡STOP .

Remember your Helping Hand Strategies:

 1. More than one answer may seem correct! Be sure to compare the choices.

 2. Read carefully and go back to the story if you are unsure.

 3. Watch for key words in the story that give you clues.

 4. Use your time wisely. If a question seems too tough, skip it and come back to it later.

---

1. Mark the word that begins with the same sound as **small**.

straw	squaw	smile	crawl
(A)	(B)	(C)	(D)

2. Which word means the opposite of **simple**?

easy	nice	similar	hard
(A)	(B)	(C)	(D)

GO ON ⇨

Read the paragraphs to help you answer questions 3–7 .

Barn Owls

Barn owls can be found all over the world. They live in grasslands, open woodlands, and farmlands where they can easily find food. Barn owls swoop over fields, listening for mice and rats. They can hear them from a quarter of a mile away! When a barn owl finds one, it drops down and catches the mouse or rat with its sharp claws. A family of barn owls can eat more than 20,000 mice and rats in a year!

A mother and father barn owl stay together for life. They make their homes in old barns and hollow trees, but they do not build nests as other birds do. The mother owl lays five to nine eggs, and they hatch about one month later.

In some places, barn owls are dying. People put poison out to chase mice away, but then the barn owls eat the sick mice. They are also having trouble finding places to lay eggs because many old trees are cut down. We should all work together to help save the barn owls.

3. How are barn owls different from other birds?

(A) They live in hollow trees.

(B) They lay many eggs.

(C) They have sharp claws.

(D) They do not build nests.

4. Which of these is not a fact from the story?

(A) In some places, barn owls are dying.

(B) Mice do not taste good.

(C) Barn owls are found all over the world.

(D) A family of barn owls can eat 20,000 mice in a year.

GO ON

5. Which is not a place that barn owls hunt?

(A) in the farmlands   (B) over rocky mountains

(C) in the grasslands   (D) over open meadows

6. What is this story mostly about?

(A) mice and rats   (B) barn owls

(C) the farmlands   (D) bird nests

7. In this story, what is the effect of cutting down trees?

(A) Barn owls have nowhere to live.

(B) They may catch on fire.

(C) They make good fire wood.

(D) They are fun to climb.

8. Which of these is probably the title of a fantasy book?

(A) My Pet Lizard   (B) My Talking Teddy

(C) My Friend Sammy   (D) My Day at Camp

9. Which of these does not belong with the others?

pencil	glue	marker	pen
(A)	(B)	(C)	(D)

10. Mark the letters that complete the word.

st_____

ip	ift	ung	uth
(A)	(B)	(C)	(D)

GO ON

Final Review Test

Read the poem to help you answer questions 11–14 .

The Day Emily Sneezed

One very hot day Emily the Elephant said, "I think I may sneeze."
  So the grassland animals said, "Excuse us, if you please."

And ran, oh they did, for they were afraid
  Of what may happen when Emily's sneeze was made.

The giraffes ran for cover and hid behind leaves
  Of the thickest and tallest of all the African trees.

The warthogs got up from feeding on their knees
  And frightfully asked, "Did Emily say she may sneeze?"

The falcon flew quickly as falcons can do.
  He remembered the last time Emily said, "Achoo!"

The earth had rumbled and all the trees shook
  Worse than any disaster you've read about in a book.

So the animals all covered their ears and closed their eyes.
  But then they got such a pleasant surprise. . .

Emily the Elephant did not let out a sneeze,
  But instead she laughed and made a cool breeze.

Now all the animals went back to their eating,
  And they were happy their land did not take a beating.

11. Where is the poem taking place?

   (A) in the rain forest   (B) in the grasslands

   (C) in the desert   (D) in the swamp

12. How do you know the giraffes were afraid of Emily's sneeze?

   (A) They hid behind trees.   (B) They shouted at Emily.

   (C) They were hot.   (D) They were hungry.

Final Review Test

13. What had caused the earth to shake?

(A) The giraffes ran to hide.

(B) The warthogs got up from their knees.

(C) Emily the Elephant's last sneeze.

(D) The falcons flew away fast.

14. What will happen the next time Emily thinks she may sneeze?

(A) The animals will laugh.   (B) The animals will hide.

(C) Emily will run and hide.   (D) There will be an earthquake.

Read the story to help you answer questions 15–17.

Gigi was excited to plant her garden. Her grandma showed her how to dig small holes for the tomato plants and cover them with dirt. Then she showed Gigi how to cut a plastic cup and put it around the stem of the tiny plant. "This will help keep worms and bugs off your plants," she said. "We should also put up a small fence to keep the rabbits out."

"Oh, I am too tired," Gigi answered.

So Gigi and her grandma went inside for some cold lemonade. Later, Gigi went to check on her plants. Something had eaten the leaves off one of her plants!

15. What do you think has eaten part of the plant?

bugs   worms   a rabbit   a butterfly
(A)   (B)   (C)   (D)

16. What would make a good title for this story?

(A) Garden Plants   (B) Tomatoes

(C) Bugs and Worms   (D) Gigi's Garden

GO ON

17. What was the first thing Gigi's grandma showed her?

(A) how to cover plants with dirt

(B) how to dig small holes

(C) how to cut a plastic cup

(D) how to put the cup around the stem

Read the story to help you answer questions 18–21.

Things Could Always Be Worse

Once upon a time, there lived a poor farmer. He shared a small house with his wife and six children. Their house was always quite noisy because the children chased each other and argued. The farmer could take it no more and went to see the wise one for help.

"You must bring your dog inside your house to live with you," said the wise one.

So the farmer did as he was told, but the noise only got worse. Now the dog was barking, and the children were arguing. The farmer went back to the wise one for the second time.

"You must bring your cow inside to live with you," said the wise one.

Again, the farmer did as the wise one said, but now the cow mooed, the dog barked, and the children argued. It was worse than ever.

The farmer continued to visit the wise one until he had his chickens, sheep, and horse living inside his house, too.

At last, the wise one told the farmer to put all of the animals back outside. When the farmer came into his house and heard only the sound of his children arguing, he thought he was very lucky to live in such a quiet house.

18. What might the wise one have told the farmer to bring in next?

his kangaroo
(A)

his lion
(B)

his bear
(C)

his pig
(D)

GO ON

19. What is the story trying to teach us?

    (A) Animals should not be loud.

    (B) Be happy with what you have.

    (C) Children should be nice.

    (D) Wise men are smart.

20. What happened after the farmer went to see the wise one the second time?

    (A) The farmer brought his chickens in to live with him.

    (B) The farmer's children stopped arguing.

    (C) The farmer put his animals back outside.

    (D) The farmer brought his cow inside.

21. What makes this story a fantasy?

    (A) Farm animals do not live inside houses.

    (B) Farmers do not have children.

    (C) Children do not argue.

    (D) Farmers do not have sheep and chickens.

22. Which of these is an opinion?

    (A) George Washington was our first president.

    (B) Our flag has 50 stars and 13 stripes.

    (C) The capital of the U.S. is Washington, D.C.

    (D) The U.S. is the best country.

GO ON

Final Review Test

23. Mark the word that fits in both sentences.

Did the phone _____? Draw a _____ around your answer.

ring   circle   bell   mark
Ⓐ   Ⓑ   Ⓒ   Ⓓ

24. Circle is to button as square is to _____.

box   sun   shirt   oval
Ⓐ   Ⓑ   Ⓒ   Ⓓ

25. Which of these could not really happen?

Ⓐ The door strangely creaked open.

Ⓑ Two strange eyes appeared in the dark.

Ⓒ The moon looked down on us and smiled.

Ⓓ A whispering sound came from the woods.

Write the title of a book you have read. Then tell about one character and the setting.

Title: _____

Character: _____

Setting: _____

Answer Key

Page 5
1. hay; 2. paint; 3. weed; 4. beet; 5. light; 6. fight; 7. paid; 8. right; 9. coat; 10. coast; 11. beads; 12. meat; 13. goat; 14. read; 15. tray

Page 6
a ray of light

1. creatures; 2. reef; 3. seaweed; 4. ray; 5. coast; 6. float; 7. eel; 8. mermaid; 9. reading; 10. beach; 11. manatee

Page 7
1. park; 2. bird; 3. barn; 4. dirt; 5. farm; 6. porch; 7. serve; 8. cord; 9. worm; 10. stork; 11. fern; 12. third; 13. girl; 14. short; 15. thirty; 16. burn; 17. purse; 18. turn; 19. fur; 20. hurt

Page 8
harebrush

chirp, birthday, squirt, curve, burn, fern, church, nurse, thirsty

Page 9
ready, yawn, broom, breakfast, faucet, pool, fawn, moose; spoon, sweater, laundry, roof, cool, read, because, shawl; saucer, shook, straw, goose, meadow, football, weather, foot

Page 10
1. cloud; 2. point; 3. tower; 4. toy; 5. screw; 6. chew; 7. news; 8. towel; 9. soil; 10. jewel; 11. cowboy; 12. mouth; 13. blouse; 14. royal; 15. growl; 16. boil

Page 11
1. clever; 2. glare; 3. chipmunk; 4. skyscraper; 5. knight; 6. whirl; 7. through; 8. floor

Page 12
Possible answers: vent, crank, gold; band, swung, strong; block, wish, west, brick, brand, bring, trash, trust, trick, trunk, sand, sank, sent, sick, sock, song, sung, sunk, sold, sing

Unit 1 Test
1. C; 2. B; 3. D; 4. B; 5. A; 6. C; 7. D; 8. A; 9. B; 10. A; 11. C; 12. D; 13. A; 14. D; 15. D; 16. C; 17. B; 18. C; 19. A; 20. C; Constructed-response answers will vary.

Page 17
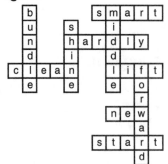

Page 18
1. D; 2. H; 3. A; 4. F; 5. C; 6. B; 7. G; 8. E; 9. I

Page 19
1. spring; 2. feet; 3. jam; 4. leaves; 5. light; 6. step; 7. kind; 8. log

Page 20
A. full moon; B. half moon; C. crescent moon; D. new moon

Page 21
1. light; 2. tool for cutting; 3. couch; 4. piece; 5. small hills; 6. special; 7. settle down

Page 22
1. refrigerator; 2. square; 3. sky; 4. horse; 5. light; 6. hose; 7. pool; 8. table

Page 23
1. yard; 2. chicken; 3. house; 4. hospital; 5. desert; 6. woods; 7. pull; 8. right; 9. hand; 10. temperature

Unit 2 Test
1. B; 2. D; 3. C; 4. C; 5. B; 6. A; 7. A; 8. D; 9. B; 10. C; 11. A; 12. C; 13. D; 14. D; 15. C; 16. A; 17. B; 18. A; 19. B; 20. D; Constructed-response answers will vary.

Page 28
Answers will vary.

Page 29
1. 1, 1; 2. 4, 35; 3. 2, 13; 4. 6, 57; 5. 5, 49; 6. 3, 21; 7. 1, 1; 8. 2, 13

Page 30
1. parallel; 2. angle; 3. point; 4. perpendicular; 5. segment; 6. ray

Page 31
1. boil; 2. carp; 3. evening; 4. icicle; 5. magnet; 6. might; 1. diet; 2. drain; 3. frisky; 4. height; 5. pickle; 6. practice

Page 32

poppy field, south

Page 33
1. Elena; 2. math; 3. Monday; 4. listening; 5. Sam; 6. Friday; 7. Monday; 8. listening; 9. Sam

Answer Key

Pages 34–35
1. The Panda Keeper; 2. Becoming a Zookeeper; 3. Caring for Hsing; 4. What Hsing Eats

Page 36
Answers will vary.

Page 37
1. C; 2. B; 3. A

Unit 3 Test
1. C; 2. D; 3. C; 4. A; 5. A; 6. B; 7. B; 8. D; 9. D; 10. B; 11. C; 12. C; 13. A; 14. D; 15. B; 16. A; 17. C; 18. D; 19. B; 20. C; Constructed-response answers will vary.

Page 43
1. banana; 2. jelly or jam; 3. wings; 4. sausage; 5. eyes

Page 44
From left to right: 4, 1, 6, 3, 5, 2

Page 45
6

Page 46
3, 7, 4, 1, 5, 2, 6

Page 47
1. Brandon was playing on Matthew's swing set.; 2. Brandon jumped from the swing set and landed in a strange way.; 3. Brandon's parents took him to the hospital.; 4. The doctor took an X ray of his arm.; 5. The boys will play tic-tac-toe.

Page 48
Answers will vary. Possible answers include: 1. First, Brandon was playing at his friend's house.; 2. Then Brandon jumped from the swing set and hurt his arm.; 3. Next, the doctor took an x-ray of Brandon's arm at the hospital.; 4. Last, Brandon and Matthew will play tic-tac-toe at recess.

Page 49
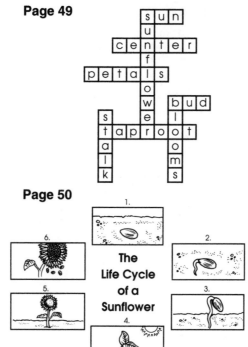

Page 50

The Life Cycle of a Sunflower

Unit 4 Test
1. C; 2. B; 3. D; 4. D; 5. C; 6. A; 7. B; 8. D; 9. A; 10. C; 11. A; 12. C; 13. B; 14. D; 15. B; 16. A; 17. C; 18. D; 19. B; 20. C; Constructed-response answers will vary.

Midway Review Test
1. D; 2. C; 3. A; 4. B; 5. D; 6. D; 7. C; 8. A; 9. B; 10. C; 11. D; 12. A; 13. B; 14. D; 15. B; 16. C; 17. D; 18. B; 19. C; 20. A; Constructed-response answers will vary.

Page 63
Answers will vary. Possible answers include: Beginning—lazy, selfish, mean; End—kind, helpful, strong

Page 64
1. proud; 2. scared; 3. worried; 4. disappointed; 5. excited

Page 65
1. City Mouse; 2. Country Mouse; 3. Country Mouse; 4. City Mouse; 5. Country Mouse; 6. City Mouse

Page 66
Answers will vary.

Page 67
Humpty Dumpty—first problem: that Humpty fell down; second problem: that they couldn't put him together again; solution: glue him together; Jack and Jill—first problem: that Jack fell down; second problem: that Jill fell down; solution: they could try again or get water from another place

Page 68
1. end, middle, beginning; 2. end, middle, beginning; 3. beginning, end, middle

Pages 69–70
Answers will vary.

Unit 5 Test
1. C; 2. B; 3. D; 4. A; 5. B; 6. C; 7. D; 8. D; 9. A; 10. A; 11. B; 12. C; 13. D; 14. A; 15. C; 16. D; 17. B; 18. C; 19. A; 20. B; Constructed-response answers will vary.

Page 77
1. C; 2. E; 3. A; 4. F; 5. D; 6. B

Page 78
Answers will vary.

Page 79
Answers will vary.

Page 80
Answers will vary. Possible answers include: 1. go to bed with gum in your mouth; 2. pick up your toys; 3. finish your work; 4. play with the copy machine

Page 81
1. S; 2. D; 3. D; 4. S

Answer Key

Page 82

Answers will vary. Possible answers include: 1. Everyone sent Mother and Father Rat to someone else.; 2. I was surprised because the noble rat did not seem special before.; 3. Water could fit through the wall. Then the wall could send the Rat Family to the sea. Then the sea could send the Rat Family back to the sun because the sun dries up water.

Page 83

Mammals: Alike—bats have fur, bats have bones like our hands, bats have skin on their wings, bats' babies drink milk and are born alive; Different—bats seem to have wings; Birds: Alike—bats have wings; Different—bats' wings are not covered with feathers, bats' wings are more like hands; mammal

Unit 6 Test

1. C; 2. C; 3. B; 4. A; 5. D; 6. D; 7. B; 8. A; 9. A; 10. D; 11. C; 12. B; 13. C; 14. D; 15. D; 16. B; 17. B; 18. A; 19. D; 20. D; Constructed-response answers will vary.

Page 91

1. fact/green; 2. fact/green; 3. opinion/blue; 4. opinion/blue; 5. fact/green; 6. opinion/blue; 7. opinion/blue

Page 92

Answers may vary. Some possible answers include: Facts: 1. Gorillas live in the mountains and forests of Zaire.; 2. Gorillas live in groups.; 3. After three years, a baby gorilla sets off on its own.; Opinions: 1. A baby gorilla does not live with his mother long enough.; 2. Gorillas eat tasty foods.; 3. We should help save gorillas' forests and mountains.

Page 93

Answers will vary.

Pages 94–95

Classifications may vary. Discuss differences in beaks.

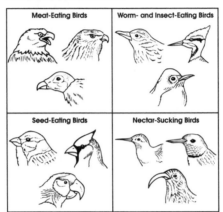

Page 96

1. potato; 2. whale; 3. road; 4. snowman; 5. shoes; 6. rock; 7. mirror; 8. lemon; 9. rocket; 10. song; 11. maple; 12. sled

Page 97

Answers will vary.

Page 98

tiger

Page 99

Zach picked the flower.; I saw Zach coming down the slide.; Zach had eaten all of the cookies.

Unit 7 Test

1. A; 2. C; 3. A; 4. D; 5. D; 6. B; 7. C; 8. D; 9. C; 10. D; 11. B; 12. B; 13. A; 14. B; 15. C; 16. B; 17. B; 18. C; 19. D; 20. B; Constructed-response answers will vary.

Page 106

1. fact; 2. fact; 3. fact; 4. fantasy; 5. fantasy; 6. fantasy; 7. fact; 8. fantasy; 9. fantasy; 10. fantasy; 11. fact; 12. fantasy; 13. fantasy; 14. fantasy; 15. fact; 16. fact

Page 107

Answers will vary.

Page 108

Answers will vary.

Page 109

Answers will vary.

Page 110

Check students' pictures.

Page 111

Check students' pictures.

Unit 8 Test

1. D; 2. A; 3. B; 4. C; 5. A; 6. B; 7. B; 8. C; 9. D; 10. A; 11. B; 12. B; 13. C; 14. D; 15. A; 16. C; 17. D; 18. B; 19. C; 20. C; Constructed-response: Check students' drawings.

Final Review Test

1. C; 2. D; 3. D; 4. B; 5. B; 6. B; 7. A; 8. B; 9. B; 10. C; 11. B; 12. A; 13. C; 14. A; 15. C; 16. D; 17. B; 18. D; 19. B; 20. D; 21. A; 22. D; 23. A; 24. A; 25. C; Constructed-response answers will vary.